Taste of Home
CHURCH SUPPERS

TASTE OF HOME BOOKS • RDA ENTHUSIAST BRANDS, LLC • MILWAUKEE, WI

Visit us at **tasteofhome.com** for other
Taste of Home books and products.

International Standard Book Number:
978-1-62145-713-8
Library of Congress Control Number:
2020949318
Component Number: 118600103H

Executive Editor: Mark Hagen
Senior Art Director: Raeann Thompson
Designer: Arielle Jardine
Deputy Editor, Copy Desk: Dulcie Shoener
Copy Editor: Sara Strauss
Contributing Editor: Michelle Rozumalski

Cover Photography:
Photographer: Mark Derse
Set Stylist: Stacey Genaw
Food Stylist: Shannon Roum

Pictured on front cover:
Pepper Jack Hash Brown Casserole, p. 49
Pictured on title page:
Key Lime Cream Pie, p. 252
Pictured on back cover:
7-Layer Gelatin Salad, p. 88
Mini Sausage Quiches, p. 23
Candy Bar Brownies, p. 232
Pictured on spine:
Garbanzo-Stuffed Mini Peppers, p. 39

Printed in USA
1 3 5 7 9 10 8 6 4 2

46

180

128

175

CONTENTS

MORE WAYS TO CONNECT WITH US:

f 🐦 📷 📌

FIND YOUR NEW GO-TO PARTY DISH

Whether you're contributing to a church supper, charity bake sale, community potluck or casual backyard barbecue, the perfect dish is at your fingertips with the 117 recipes in this new cookbook from the *Taste of Home* editors.

100

Get ready for bring-a-dish success when your buffet contribution garners the most attention and you come home with an empty platter. It's easy with recipes from this large-print edition of **Taste of Home Church Suppers,** a cookbook for anyone looking to feed a group. Dig into crowd-pleasing appetizers, salads and sides, as well entrees, sub sandwiches and soups that serve 8, 10, 20 or more. And, of course, you'll find a bevy of lip-smacking sweets, too!

Organizing a pancake breakfast or family reunion? This book has you covered with all the recipes you need. Maybe you're simply looking for a few bites to round out this year's Easter brunch, backyard barbecue, Christmas dinner or New Year's bash—you'll find dozens of new favorites here. Take cookie exchanges to new heights, bake memorable food gifts, and surprise family and friends with mouthwatering on-the-go dishes all year long!

144

218

222

GRAB AND GO WITH THESE MAKE-&-TAKE TIPS

The recipes found here make it easy to find the perfect potluck contribution. Consider these handy hints to be sure your dish arrives in terrific condition.

Build a DIY Multilevel Tote

If you have more dishes than hands, reach for a cooling rack with folding legs. Fold out the legs and use the rack to create sturdy, stable levels inside a carrying tote without crushing what's below. You can also build layers by propping a sheet pan with ring molds or cans.

Ensure a No-Slip Trip

Place grippy drawer liners or silicone baking mats in the car before loading your food. The liners will keep dishes from sliding and contain any errant spills. An old yoga mat works well for this, too.

Keep a Lid on It

Use a bungee cord, painter's tape or a thick ribbon to keep the lid of your slow cooker or Dutch oven in place. Secure the cord around the handles and over the top. Now you're ready to transport without risk of a mess.

Bring a Salad

You can serve a crisp salad when you're far from home. Bring the fixings in a serving bowl along with the utensils. Toss it all together at your destination.

Frosting Is Good Glue

If you're transporting a cake to a special event, make it easier to tote with this little tip: Secure the cake (or cardboard cake circle, if you're using one) onto the presentation plate with a dab of frosting. This makes the cake less likely to slide around, even if you have to brake suddenly.

Pack a Touch-Up Kit

Make a little touch-up kit of decorations and frosting (just in case) to take with your decorated cake. Pack the items with a clean dish towel and offset spatula. Take the frosting in its pastry bag if you used one.

Make a Plan for Safety

If you're organizing a church supper or large potluck, keep foods safe with these tips.

- Set up in the shade. If possible, keep the outdoor buffet in a cool area—like in a garage, in the shade of a building or under a big tree. Stash coolers in the shade to keep drinks colder, too.

- Have plenty of ice to pack around dishes and keep things cold. Not only will the food taste a bit better when it's properly chilled, but you won't have to worry about the risk of any foodborne illnesses.

- Likewise, keep hot foods hot. Foods should not be out at room temperature for more than 2 hours (less if it's hotter than that). Chafing dishes, slow cookers, and grills or ovens set on low help to keep things safe.

- Designate a meal time. Set aside 2 hours for the meal, and serve hot and cold foods only during that time. Afterward, put leftovers in the fridge or pack them in well-iced coolers.

MINI SAUSAGE
QUICHES, 23

CHAPTER 1

APPETIZERS & SNACKS

From saucy meatballs to irresistible dips, the small bites in this chapter are guaranteed to go over big with the crowd.

HOT CHEESE DIP

When a colleague brought this golden baked dip to school for a teachers potluck, I immediately gave It an A+. I just had to have the recipe for this wonderfully creamy dish!
—*Ardyce Piehl, Poynette, WI*

TAKES: 30 min. • **MAKES:** 3 cups

2 cups shredded part-skim mozzarella cheese
2 cups shredded cheddar cheese
2 cups mayonnaise
1 medium onion, minced
1 can (4 to 4½ oz.) chopped green chiles, drained
½ cup sliced ripe olives
1½ oz. sliced pepperoni
Assorted crackers and fresh vegetables

Preheat oven to 325°. Combine the first 5 ingredients; spread into a greased shallow baking dish or pie plate. Top with olives and pepperoni. Bake until bubbly, about 25 minutes. Serve with crackers and fresh vegetables.

2 Tbsp.: 201 cal., 19g fat (5g sat. fat), 18mg chol., 285mg sod., 2g carb. (0 sugars, 0 fiber), 5g pro.

READER RAVE

"Our family loves this snack. We cut the pepperoni into small bits and stir it in before cooking. There's never an issue with the dip disappearing when we make it."

—GINGERRAE, TASTEOFHOME.COM

SUN-DRIED TOMATO GOAT CHEESE EMPANADAS

I created my own appetizer because I entertain a lot and wanted something simple but special. People like these empanadas so much! I always make extra.
—*Lynn Scully, Rancho Santa Fe, CA*

PREP: 1 hour • **BAKE:** 15 min. • **MAKES:** about 1½ dozen

1 Tbsp. olive oil

1 medium sweet onion, halved and thinly sliced

1 log (4 oz.) fresh goat cheese, crumbled

¼ cup finely chopped oil-packed sun-dried tomatoes, drained

Pastry for a single-crust pie (9 in.) or 1 sheet refrigerated pie crust

1. In a large skillet, heat oil over medium heat. Add sweet onion; cook and stir until softened, 4-5 minutes. Reduce heat to medium-low; cook, stirring occasionally, until deep golden brown, 30-40 minutes. Remove from heat. Let cool slightly. Gently stir in goat cheese and tomatoes.

2. Preheat oven to 400°. On a lightly floured surface, roll dough to ¼-in. thickness. Cut with a floured 3-in. round biscuit cutter. Place pastry circles 2 in. apart on baking sheets. Place 1 heaping tsp. of filling on 1 side of each circle. Brush edges of pastry with water; fold circles in half. With a fork, press edges to seal. Bake until golden brown, 15-20 minutes.

1 empanada: 99 cal., 7g fat (4g sat. fat), 18mg chol., 98mg sod., 8g carb. (0 sugars, 0 fiber), 2g pro.

Pastry for a single-crust pie (9 in.): Combine 1¼ cups all-purpose flour and ¼ tsp. salt; cut in ½ cup cold butter until crumbly. Gradually add 3-5 Tbsp. ice water, tossing with a fork until dough holds together when pressed. Cover and refrigerate 1 hour.

PICNIC FRUIT PUNCH

This rosy cooler is so refreshing on warm days. Before trying it, some people think it's pink lemonade. They're pleasantly surprised when they taste the tangy blend of cranberry, pineapple, orange and lemon juices.

—*Marion Lowery, Medford, OR*

PREP: 10 min. + chilling • **MAKES:** 5 qt.

8 cups cranberry juice
3 cups pineapple juice
3 cups orange juice
¼ cup lemon juice
1 liter ginger ale, chilled
1 medium navel orange, sliced

In a large container, combine the juices; refrigerate. Just before serving, transfer to a punch bowl; stir in ginger ale and orange slices.

1 cup: 106 cal., 0 fat (0 sat. fat), 0 chol., 6mg sod., 27g carb. (26g sugars, 0 fiber), 1g pro.

READER RAVE

"This is my go-to recipe for any summer get-together. Everyone loves this bubbly, thirst-quenching drink!"

—KELSEYPOWER_05, TASTEOFHOME.COM

SWEET & TANGY CHICKEN WINGS

I love the convenience of slow-cooker recipes for get-togethers.
Start these wings a few hours ahead of time and you'll have
fantastic appetizers ready when your guests arrive!
—Ida Tuey, South Lyon, MI

PREP: 20 min. • **COOK:** 2¼ hours • **MAKES:** 2 dozen

12 chicken wings
    (about 3 lbs.)
½ tsp. salt, divided
    Dash pepper
1½ cups ketchup
¼ cup packed brown sugar
¼ cup red wine vinegar
2 Tbsp. Worcestershire
    sauce
1 Tbsp. Dijon mustard
1 tsp. minced garlic
1 tsp. liquid smoke, optional
    Optional: Sliced jalapeno
    peppers, finely chopped
    red onion and sesame
    seeds

1. Using a sharp knife, cut through the 2 wing joints; discard wingtips. Sprinkle chicken with a dash of salt and pepper. Broil 4-6 in. from heat until golden brown, 6-8 minutes on each side. Transfer to a greased 5-qt. slow cooker.

2. Combine the ketchup, brown sugar, red wine vinegar, Worcestershire, mustard, garlic, liquid smoke if desired, and remaining salt; pour over wings. Toss to coat.

3. Cover and cook on low until the chicken is tender, 2-3 hours. If desired, top with jalapenos, onion and sesame seeds to serve.

Freeze option: Freeze cooled fully cooked chicken wings in freezer containers. To use, partially thaw in refrigerator overnight. Reheat in a foil-lined 15x10x1-in. baking pan in a preheated 325° oven until heated through, covering if necessary to prevent browning. Serve as directed.

1 piece: 74 cal., 3g fat (1g sat. fat), 14mg chol., 282mg sod., 7g carb. (6g sugars, 0 fiber), 5g pro.

SAUSAGE WONTON STARS

These fancy little cups are ideal for large groups. Cute and crunchy, the wontons
are stuffed with a cheesy pork sausage filling that people of all ages enjoy.
We keep a few stars in the freezer to reheat for late-night snacking.
—*Mary Thomas, North Lewisburg, OH*

TAKES: 30 min. • **MAKES:** 4 dozen

1 pkg. (12 oz.) wonton wrappers
1 lb. bulk pork sausage
2 cups shredded Colby cheese
½ medium green pepper, chopped
½ medium sweet red pepper, chopped
2 bunches green onions, sliced
½ cup ranch salad dressing

1. Preheat oven to 350°. Lightly press wonton wrappers onto the bottoms and up the sides of greased miniature muffin cups. Bake until the edges are browned, about 5 minutes.

2. In a large skillet, cook the sausage over medium heat until no longer pink, breaking into crumbles; drain. Stir in the cheese, peppers, onions and salad dressing. Spoon a rounded Tbsp. into each wonton cup. Bake until heated through, 6-7 minutes.

1 appetizer: 69 cal., 5g fat (2g sat. fat), 10mg chol., 143mg sod., 4g carb. (0 sugars, 0 fiber), 3g pro.

SPINACH TURNOVERS

The flaky cream cheese pastry adds sensational texture to these
hot appetizers—and just wait until you taste the yummy filling! I usually
fix a double batch and freeze some to have on hand for unexpected guests.

—Jean von Bereghy, Oconomowoc, WI

. . . .

PREP: 30 min. + chilling • **BAKE:** 10 min. • **MAKES:** about 4 dozen

2   pkg. (8 oz. each)
      cream cheese, softened
¾   cup butter, softened
2½ cups all-purpose flour
½   tsp. salt

FILLING

5   bacon strips, diced
¼   cup finely chopped onion
2   garlic cloves, minced
1   pkg. (10 oz.) frozen
      chopped spinach,
      thawed and well drained
1   cup 4% cottage cheese
¼   tsp. salt
¼   tsp. pepper
⅛   tsp. ground nutmeg
1   large egg, beaten
      Salsa, optional

1. In a bowl, beat cream cheese and butter until smooth.
Combine flour and salt; gradually add to creamed mixture
(dough will be stiff). Turn onto a floured surface; gently
knead 10 times. Cover and refrigerate at least 2 hours.

2. In a skillet, cook bacon until crisp. Remove bacon;
reserve 1 Tbsp. drippings. Saute onion and garlic in
drippings until tender. Remove from the heat; stir in
bacon, spinach, cottage cheese and seasonings. Cool.

3. On a lightly floured surface, roll the dough to ⅛-in.
thickness. Cut into 3-in. circles; brush edges with egg.
Place 1 heaping tsp. of filling on each circle. Fold over;
seal edges. Prick tops with a fork. Brush with egg.

4. Bake at 400° for 10-12 minutes or until golden brown.
Serve with salsa if desired.

1 turnover: 103 cal., 8g fat (4g sat. fat), 23mg chol.,
129mg sod., 6g carb. (1g sugars, 0 fiber), 2g pro.

MEATBALLS WITH CHIMICHURRI SAUCE

Liven up packaged frozen meatballs by combining fresh cilantro, garlic and more in a South American herb sauce. Make sure to offer some on the side for dipping!
—*Amy Chase, Vanderhoof, BC*

TAKES: 30 min. • **MAKES:** about 20 (⅔ cup sauce)

1 pkg. (22 oz.) frozen fully cooked Angus beef meatballs
3 garlic cloves, peeled
1 cup packed Italian flat leaf parsley
¼ cup packed fresh cilantro leaves
1 tsp. salt
¼ tsp. coarsely ground pepper
2 Tbsp. red wine vinegar
½ cup extra virgin olive oil

1. Prepare meatballs according to package directions.

2. Meanwhile, place garlic in a small food processor; pulse until chopped. Add parsley, cilantro, salt and pepper; pulse until finely chopped. Add red wine vinegar. While processing, gradually add oil in a steady stream.

3. In a large bowl, toss meatballs with a little more than half of the chimichurri sauce. Transfer to a platter. Serve with remaining sauce for dipping.

1 meatball with about 2 tsp. sauce: 130 cal., 12g fat (4g sat. fat), 17mg chol., 318mg sod., 2g carb. (0 sugars, 0 fiber), 4g pro.

MINI SAUSAGE QUICHES

Crescent roll dough makes it oh-so-easy to prepare these delightful bites loaded with sausage and cheese. Serve the cute quiches for brunch or any potluck gathering.
—Jan Mead, Milford, CT

PREP: 25 min. • **BAKE:** 20 min. • **MAKES:** 4 dozen

½ lb. bulk hot Italian sausage
2 Tbsp. dried minced onion
2 Tbsp. minced chives
1 tube (8 oz.) refrigerated crescent rolls
4 large eggs, lightly beaten
2 cups shredded Swiss cheese
1 cup 4% cottage cheese
⅓ cup grated Parmesan cheese
Paprika
Additional minced chives, optional

1. In a large skillet, brown sausage and onion over medium heat until meat is no longer pink, 4-5 minutes, breaking sausage into crumbles; drain. Stir in chives.

2. On a lightly floured surface, unroll crescent roll dough into a long rectangle; seal the seams and perforations. Cut into 48 pieces. Press onto the bottoms and up the sides of greased miniature muffin cups.

3. Fill each with about 2 tsp. sausage mixture. In a large bowl, combine eggs and cheeses. Spoon 2 tsp. over sausage mixture in each cup. Sprinkle with paprika.

4. Bake at 375° until a knife inserted in the center comes out clean, 20-25 minutes. Cool for 5 minutes before removing from pans to wire racks. If desired, sprinkle with additional minced chives. Serve warm.

1 mini quiche: 66 cal., 5g fat (2g sat. fat), 27mg chol., 116mg sod., 2g carb. (1g sugars, 0 fiber), 4g pro.

TEST KITCHEN TIP

Make these gluten free by simply skipping the crescent roll crust.

MARINATED OLIVE & CHEESE RING

We love to make our Italian meals into celebrations, and an antipasto always kicks things off. This one is almost too pretty to eat, especially when sprinkled with pimientos, fresh basil and parsley.

—*Patricia Harmon, Baden, PA*

PREP: 25 min. + chilling • **MAKES:** 16 servings

- 1 pkg. (8 oz.) cream cheese, cold
- 1 pkg. (10 oz.) sharp white cheddar cheese, cut into ¼-in. slices
- ⅓ cup pimiento-stuffed olives
- ⅓ cup pitted Greek olives
- ¼ cup balsamic vinegar
- ¼ cup olive oil
- 1 Tbsp. minced fresh parsley
- 1 Tbsp. minced fresh basil or 1 tsp. dried basil
- 2 garlic cloves, minced
- 1 jar (2 oz.) pimiento strips, drained and chopped
- Toasted French bread baguette slices

1. Cut cream cheese lengthwise in half; cut each half into ¼-in. slices. On a serving plate, arrange cheeses upright in a ring, alternating cheddar and cream cheese slices. Place olives in center.

2. In a small bowl, whisk vinegar, oil, parsley, basil and garlic until blended; drizzle over cheeses and olives. Sprinkle with pimientos. Refrigerate, covered, at least 8 hours or overnight. Serve with baguette slices.

1 serving: 168 cal., 16g fat (7g sat. fat), 34mg chol., 260mg sod., 2g carb. (1g sugars, 0 fiber), 6g pro.

TEST KITCHEN TIP

This rustic starter is super adaptable. Any cheeses will work in place of the cream cheese and sharp cheddar—just keep the overall weight the same. For even more variety, fold thin slices of deli cuts, such as pepperoni and salami, in half and tuck them between the cheese slices.

FIVE-SPICE CHICKEN WINGS

These tongue-tingling wings are baked to a perfect golden brown and feature mild Asian spices. Thanks to an overnight marinade, the chicken inside stays tender while the skin has an irresistible crunch.
—*Crystal Jo Bruns, Iliff, CO*

PREP: 20 min. + marinating • **BAKE:** 25 min. • **MAKES:** about 3 dozen

3½ lbs. chicken wings
3 green onions, chopped
2 Tbsp. sweet chili sauce
2 Tbsp. reduced-sodium soy sauce
2 Tbsp. fish sauce or additional soy sauce
4 garlic cloves, minced
1 Tbsp. sugar
1 Tbsp. Chinese five-spice powder
2 medium limes, cut into wedges

1. Cut chicken wings into 3 sections; discard wingtip sections. Combine the green onions, chili sauce, soy sauce, fish sauce, garlic, sugar and five-spice powder in a large container. Add wings and toss to coat. Cover and refrigerate 8 hours or overnight.

2. Drain chicken, discarding the marinade. Place wings in a greased 15x10x1-in. baking pan.

3. Bake at 425° for 25-30 minutes or until the chicken is no longer pink, turning every 10 minutes. Squeeze lime wedges over wings.

1 piece: 52 cal., 3g fat (1g sat. fat), 14mg chol., 81mg sod., 1g carb. (0 sugars, 0 fiber), 5g pro.

BUFFALO WING BITES

The Buffalo wing fans in my family were happy to do the taste testing as I was experimenting to create these zingy snacks. This version was the winner!
—*Jasey McBurnett, Rock Springs, WY*

PREP: 25 min. • **BAKE:** 15 min. • **MAKES:** 2 dozen (2 cups dressing)

2 Tbsp. grated Parmesan cheese
1 envelope ranch salad dressing mix, divided
1 cup mayonnaise
1 cup 2% milk
¼ cup crumbled blue cheese, optional
1¼ cups finely chopped cooked chicken breast
1¼ cups shredded cheddar-Monterey Jack cheese
¼ cup Buffalo wing sauce
1 tube (13.8 oz.) refrigerated pizza crust
2 Tbsp. butter, melted

1. Preheat oven to 400°. In a small bowl, combine Parmesan cheese and 1 tsp. dressing mix. In another bowl, mix mayonnaise, milk and remaining dressing mix. If desired, stir in blue cheese. Refrigerate until serving.

2. In a large bowl, mix the chicken, cheddar-Monterey Jack cheese and wing sauce. On a lightly floured surface, unroll pizza dough and pat into a 14x12-in. rectangle. Cut into 24 squares.

3. Place 1 rounded Tbsp. chicken mixture on the center of each square. Pull corners together to enclose filling; pinch to seal. Place 1 in. apart on greased baking sheets, seam side down. Brush tops with butter; sprinkle with Parmesan cheese mixture.

4. Bake 15-17 minutes or until golden brown. Serve with dressing.

1 appetizer: 165 cal., 12g fat (3g sat. fat), 18mg chol., 374mg sod., 9g carb. (1g sugars, 0 fiber), 5g pro.

DILLY MINI CHEESE BALLS

Here's a downsized variation of the traditional cheese ball. Shaped into single bites, these are fun and easy to eat with pretzel sticks or crackers.
—Carole Lanthier, Courtice, ON

PREP: 15 min. + chilling • **MAKES:** 2½ dozen

1 pkg. (8 oz.) cream cheese, softened
1½ cups sharp shredded cheddar cheese
½ cup chopped dill pickles
2 green onions, finely chopped
2 Tbsp. mayonnaise
1 tsp. Worcestershire sauce
1 cup chopped walnuts
¼ cup minced fresh parsley
   Pretzel sticks or assorted crackers

In a small mixing bowl, combine the first 6 ingredients. Shape tablespoons of cheese mixture into balls. Roll in nuts and parsley. Cover and refrigerate for 20 minutes before serving. Serve with pretzel sticks or crackers.

1 mini cheese ball: 56 cal., 5g fat (2g sat. fat), 10mg chol., 65mg sod., 1g carb. (0 sugars, 0 fiber), 2g pro.

TEST KITCHEN TIP

If the cream cheese mixture is too soft to shape into balls right after mixing, cover and chill for 30 minutes before shaping.

BOURBON CANDIED BACON DEVILED EGGS

At our house, it doesn't get any better than a big platter of deviled eggs with bacon—bourbon candied bacon, that is. See if you can resist them!
—*Colleen Delawder, Herndon, VA*

PREP: 20 min. • **BAKE:** 25 min. • **MAKES:** 2 dozen

2 Tbsp. brown sugar
¾ tsp. Dijon mustard
½ tsp. maple syrup
⅛ tsp. salt
2 tsp. bourbon, optional
4 thick-sliced bacon strips

EGGS
12 hard-boiled large eggs
¾ cup mayonnaise
1 Tbsp. maple syrup
1 Tbsp. Dijon mustard
¼ tsp. pepper
¼ tsp. ground chipotle pepper
Minced fresh chives

1. Preheat oven to 350°. In a small bowl, mix brown sugar, ¾ tsp. mustard, ½ tsp. syrup and salt. If desired, stir in bourbon. Coat bacon with brown sugar mixture. Place on a rack in a foil-lined 15x10x1-in. baking pan. Bake 25-30 minutes or until crisp. Cool completely.

2. Cut eggs in half lengthwise. Remove yolks, reserving whites. In a small bowl, mash yolks. Add mayonnaise, 1 Tbsp. syrup, 1 Tbsp. mustard and both types of pepper; stir until smooth. Chop bacon finely; fold half into the egg yolk mixture. Spoon or pipe into egg whites. Sprinkle with the remaining bacon and the chives. Refrigerate, covered, until serving.

1 stuffed egg half: 107 cal., 9g fat (2g sat. fat), 97mg chol., 142mg sod., 2g carb. (2g sugars, 0 fiber), 4g pro.

TURKEY & SWISS BISCUIT SLIDERS

One of my favorite things to whip up in the kitchen is homemade buttermilk biscuits. Simple sandwiches are a wonderful way to showcase these melt-in-your-mouth treats.
—*Cindy Esposito, Bloomfield, NJ*

PREP: 35 min. + rising • **BAKE:** 10 min. • **MAKES:** 16 sliders

1 pkg. (¼ oz.) active dry yeast
⅔ cup warm buttermilk (110° to 115°)
2 Tbsp. warm water (110° to 115°)
2 cups bread flour
3 Tbsp. sugar
1½ tsp. baking powder
½ tsp. salt
½ cup shortening
¾ lb. thinly sliced deli smoked turkey
½ lb. sliced Swiss cheese
  Dijon mustard, optional

1. In a small bowl, dissolve yeast in warm buttermilk and water. Place the flour, sugar, baking powder and salt in a food processor; pulse until blended. Add the shortening; pulse until shortening is the size of peas. While processing, gradually add yeast mixture and process just until dough forms a ball.

2. Turn the dough onto a lightly floured surface; knead 8-10 times. Pat or roll dough to ½-in. thickness; cut with a floured 2-in. biscuit cutter. Place 2 in. apart on greased baking sheets. Let rise until almost doubled, about 30 minutes.

3. Preheat oven to 425°. Bake the biscuits 7-9 minutes or until golden brown. Remove to wire racks to cool slightly. Preheat broiler.

4. Split biscuits in half; place bottoms on greased baking sheets. Layer with turkey and cheese. Broil 3-4 in. from heat 2-3 minutes or until cheese is melted. Replace tops. If desired, serve with mustard.

1 slider: 198 cal., 11g fat (5g sat. fat), 23mg chol., 306mg sod., 14g carb. (3g sugars, 0 fiber), 11g pro.

CHILES RELLENOS SQUARES

A friend shared this variation of chiles rellenos, and now my family requests it all the time. Cut the zippy squares into larger pieces if you'd like a side dish instead.
—Fran Carll, Long Beach, CA

PREP: 10 min. • **BAKE:** 25 min. • **MAKES:** 16 servings

3 cups shredded
  Monterey Jack cheese
1½ cups shredded
  cheddar cheese
2 cans (4 oz. each) chopped
  green chiles, drained
2 large eggs
2 Tbsp. 2% milk
1 Tbsp. all-purpose flour

1. Preheat oven to 375°. Sprinkle half of each cheese onto the bottom of a greased 8-in. square baking dish. Layer with chiles and remaining cheeses.

2. Whisk together eggs, milk and flour; pour over the top. Bake, uncovered, until set, 25-30 minutes. Cool 15 minutes before cutting.

1 piece: 130 cal., 10g fat (7g sat. fat), 57mg chol., 214mg sod., 1g carb. (0 sugars, 0 fiber), 8g pro.

READER RAVE

"Easy and fantastic. I have a recipe for shrimp rellenos, but it's time-consuming. Using a bag of shredded Mexican cheese blend made this recipe even simpler. Definitely will make again."

—BUTCHER2BOY, TASTEOFHOME.COM

GARBANZO-STUFFED MINI PEPPERS

Mini peppers are so colorful and are the perfect size for a two-bite appetizer.
They have all the crunch of a pita chip—without the extra calories!
—*Christine Hanover, Lewiston, CA*

TAKES: 20 min. • **MAKES:** 32 appetizers

1 tsp. cumin seeds
1 can (15 oz.) garbanzo beans or chickpeas, rinsed and drained
¼ cup fresh cilantro leaves
3 Tbsp. water
3 Tbsp. cider vinegar
¼ tsp. salt
16 miniature sweet peppers, halved lengthwise
Additional fresh cilantro leaves

1. In a dry small skillet, toast cumin seeds over medium heat until aromatic, 1-2 minutes, stirring frequently. Transfer to a food processor. Add garbanzo beans, cilantro, water, vinegar and salt; pulse until blended.

2. Spoon into pepper halves. Top with additional cilantro. Refrigerate until serving.

1 appetizer: 15 cal., 0 fat (0 sat. fat), 0 chol., 36mg sod., 3g carb. (1g sugars, 1g fiber), 1g pro.

TEST KITCHEN TIP

Running short on time? Mix up the filling and serve it with crackers or veggies for dipping.

SHEET-PAN BACON & EGGS BREAKFAST, 61

CHAPTER 2

BREAKFAST FOR A BUNCH

Need a crowd-sized dish in the morning? Whip up these eye-openers without having to rise at the break of dawn!

CARAMELIZED BACON TWISTS

Whenever my grandchildren come over, these sweet chewy bacon strips are a must. Lining the pan with foil before baking helps cut down on cleanup.
—*Jane Paschke, University Parkway, FL*

TAKES: 30 min. • **MAKES:** about 3 dozen

½ cup packed brown sugar
2 tsp. ground cinnamon
1 lb. bacon strips

1. Preheat oven to 350°. Line a 15x10x1-in. pan with foil.

2. In a shallow bowl, mix brown sugar and cinnamon. Cut bacon strips crosswise in half; dip in sugar mixture to coat. Twist 2 or 3 times, then place in prepared pan. Bake until browned and crisp, 15-20 minutes.

Freeze option: Freeze the cooled bacon twists in freezer containers, separating layers with waxed paper. If desired, reheat in a microwave oven or on a foil-lined baking sheet in a preheated 350° oven before serving.

1 bacon twist: 35 cal., 2g fat (1g sat. fat), 5mg chol., 81mg sod., 3g carb. (3g sugars, 0 fiber), 2g pro.

STRAWBERRY-HAZELNUT FRENCH TOAST

When my husband and I discovered this at a bed-and-breakfast in Arkansas, we bought the inn's cookbook so we could enjoy the same treat at home. We've changed the recipe a bit since then, but it still reminds us of that lovely B&B.

—*Lynn Daniel, Dallas, TX*

PREP: 15 min. + chilling • **BAKE:** 35 min. • **MAKES:** 10 servings

½   cup butter, cubed
1   cup packed brown sugar
2   Tbsp. light corn syrup
10   slices French bread baguette (1 in. thick)
5   large eggs
1½   cups half-and-half cream
2   Tbsp. hazelnut liqueur or hazelnut flavoring syrup
1   Tbsp. vanilla extract
   Sliced fresh strawberries and chopped hazelnuts

1. In a microwave, melt butter with brown sugar and light corn syrup; stir until brown sugar is blended. Pour into a greased 13x9-in. baking dish; top with bread.

2. In a large bowl, whisk the eggs, cream, liqueur and vanilla; pour over bread. Refrigerate, covered, overnight.

3. Preheat oven to 350°. Remove French toast from refrigerator while oven heats. Bake, uncovered, until the top is puffed, the edges are golden and a knife inserted in the center comes out clean, 35-40 minutes. Let stand 5-10 minutes before serving. Serve with strawberries and hazelnuts.

1 slice: 304 cal., 15g fat (9g sat. fat), 135mg chol., 184mg sod., 34g carb. (29g sugars, 0 fiber), 5g pro.

HEAVENLY CHEESE DANISH

This homemade Danish is baked to flaky perfection and gets its glossy look from a simple egg wash. The result is just as divine as any pastry in a bakery or coffee shop.

—Josephine Triton, Lakewood, OH

PREP: 50 min. + chilling • **BAKE:** 15 min. • **MAKES:** 16 rolls

2 pkg. (¼ oz. each) active dry yeast
½ cup warm water (110° to 115°)
4 cups all-purpose flour
⅓ cup sugar
2 tsp. salt
1 cup cold butter, cubed
1 cup 2% milk
4 large egg yolks, room temperature

ASSEMBLY

3 tsp. ground cinnamon, divided
12 oz. cream cheese, softened
⅓ cup sugar
1 large egg, separated, room temperature
1 Tbsp. water
2 Tbsp. maple syrup

1. Dissolve the yeast in warm water. In another bowl, mix flour, sugar and salt; cut in butter until crumbly. Add milk, egg yolks and yeast mixture; stir to form a soft dough (the dough will be sticky). Cover and refrigerate 8-24 hours.

2. To assemble, punch down dough; divide into 4 portions. On a lightly floured surface, pat each portion into a 9x4-in. rectangle; sprinkle each with ¾ tsp. cinnamon. Cut each rectangle lengthwise into four 9x1-in. strips. Twist each strip, then loosely wrap strip around itself to form a coil; tuck end under and pinch to seal. Place 3 in. apart on greased baking sheets.

3. Beat cream cheese, sugar and egg yolk until smooth. Press an indentation in the center of each roll; fill with 1 rounded Tbsp. cream cheese mixture. Cover; let rise in a warm place until doubled, about 45 minutes. Preheat oven to 350°.

4. Whisk egg white with water; brush over the rolls. Bake until golden brown, 15-20 minutes. Remove to wire racks; brush with syrup. Serve warm. Refrigerate leftovers.

1 roll: 359 cal., 21g fat (12g sat. fat), 111mg chol., 468mg sod., 37g carb. (12g sugars, 1g fiber), 7g pro.

PEPPER JACK HASH BROWN CASSEROLE

I found myself in need of a last-minute potato dish, but I had no potatoes. Frozen hash browns and the cheeses in my freezer provided the perfect solution.
—*Cyndy Gerken, Naples, FL*

PREP: 25 min. • **BAKE:** 25 min. • **MAKES:** 12 servings

1 pkg. (30 oz.) frozen shredded hash brown potatoes, thawed

1 can (10½ oz.) condensed cream of chicken soup, undiluted

2 cups shredded pepper jack cheese

1½ cups heavy whipping cream

½ cup butter, melted

½ cup sour cream

¼ cup shredded Parmesan cheese

½ tsp. salt

½ tsp. onion powder

¼ tsp. garlic powder

¼ tsp. pepper

TOPPING

1 cup crushed potato chips

5 bacon strips, cooked and crumbled

¾ cup shredded Parmesan cheese

1 tsp. paprika

1. Preheat oven to 350°. In a large bowl, combine first 11 ingredients. Transfer to a greased 13x9-in. baking dish. For topping, combine the potato chips, bacon and Parmesan; sprinkle over casserole. Top with paprika.

2. Bake, uncovered, until edges are bubbly and topping is golden brown, 25-30 minutes.

⅔ cup: 416 cal., 33g fat (19g sat. fat), 87mg chol., 682mg sod., 20g carb. (2g sugars, 2g fiber), 12g pro.

READER RAVE

"This was so easy to prepare and absolutely delicious! The variety of textures and the kick from the pepper jack cheese made it really special."
—TERESAWITT, TASTEOFHOME.COM

SAGE TURKEY SAUSAGE PATTIES

When you want to cut salt and saturated fat, turkey sausage is a terrific option. The aroma of these patties sizzling in the pan will wake up any sleepyhead.
—*Sharman Schubert, Seattle, WA*

TAKES: 30 min. • **MAKES:** 12 servings

¼ cup grated
Parmesan cheese
3 Tbsp. minced
fresh parsley or 1 Tbsp.
dried parsley flakes
2 Tbsp. fresh sage or
2 tsp. dried sage leaves
2 garlic cloves, minced
1 tsp. fennel seed, crushed
¾ tsp. salt
½ tsp. pepper
1½ lbs. lean ground turkey
1 Tbsp. olive oil

1. In a large bowl, combine the first 7 ingredients. Crumble ground turkey over mixture and mix well. Shape into twelve 3-in. patties.

2. In a large skillet, cook the patties in oil in batches over medium heat for 3-5 minutes on each side or until meat is no longer pink. Drain on paper towels if necessary.

Freeze option: Place patties on a waxed paper-lined baking sheet; cover and freeze until firm. Remove from pan and transfer to a resealable freezer container. To use, place patties on a baking sheet coated with cooking spray. Bake in a preheated 350° oven 15 minutes on each side or until heated through.

1 patty: 104 cal., 6g fat (2g sat. fat), 46mg chol., 227mg sod., 0 carb. (0 sugars, 0 fiber), 11g pro.
Diabetic exchanges: 1 lean meat, 1 fat.

CRANBERRY CREAM CHEESE FRENCH TOAST

For brunch, a friend made this overnight French toast with blueberries.
I make my own version with cranberry sauce. Either way, it's wonderful!
—*Sandie Heindel, Liberty, MO*

PREP: 25 min. + chilling • **BAKE:** 50 min. + standing • **MAKES:** 12 servings

12 cups cubed French bread (about 12 oz.)
2   pkg. (8 oz. each) cream cheese, cubed
1   can (14 oz.) whole-berry cranberry sauce
12 large eggs, lightly beaten
2   cups 2% milk
⅓   cup maple syrup
2   tsp. ground cinnamon
    Dash ground nutmeg
    Additional maple syrup, optional

1. Arrange half the bread in a single layer in a greased 13x9-in. baking dish; top with the cream cheese and spoonfuls of cranberry sauce. Top with remaining bread.

2. In a large bowl, whisk eggs, milk, ⅓ cup maple syrup, cinnamon and nutmeg until blended. Pour over casserole. Refrigerate, covered, overnight.

3. Remove the casserole from refrigerator 30 minutes before baking. Preheat oven to 350°. Bake, uncovered, until a knife inserted in the center comes out clean, 50-60 minutes. Let stand 10 minutes before serving. If desired, serve with additional maple syrup.

1 serving: 375 cal., 19g fat (10g sat. fat), 231mg chol., 382mg sod., 38g carb. (18g sugars, 1g fiber), 13g pro.

PIGS IN A POOL

My children love sausages and pancakes, but making that breakfast on a busy weekday was out of the question. These pigs-in-a-blanket spinoffs have the same kid appeal, freeze like a dream and reheat in seconds.
—*Lisa Dodd, Greenville, SC*

PREP: 45 min. • **BAKE:** 20 min. • **MAKES:** 4 dozen

1 lb. reduced-fat bulk pork sausage
2 cups all-purpose flour
¼ cup sugar
1 Tbsp. baking powder
1 tsp. salt
½ tsp. ground cinnamon
¼ tsp. ground nutmeg
1 large egg, room temperature, lightly beaten
2 cups fat-free milk
2 Tbsp. canola oil
2 Tbsp. honey
    Maple syrup, optional

1. Preheat oven to 350°. Coat 48 mini muffin cups with cooking spray.

2. Shape pork sausage into forty-eight ¾-in. balls. Place meatballs on a rack coated with cooking spray in a shallow baking pan. Bake until cooked through, 15-20 minutes. Drain on paper towels.

3. In a large bowl, whisk flour, sugar, baking powder, salt and spices. In another bowl, whisk egg, milk, oil and honey until blended. Add to flour mixture; stir just until moistened.

4. Place a sausage ball in each mini muffin cup; cover with batter. Bake until lightly browned, 20-25 minutes. Cool 5 minutes before removing from pans to wire racks. Serve warm, with syrup if desired.

Freeze option: Freeze cooled muffins in airtight freezer containers. To use, microwave each muffin on high until heated through, 20-30 seconds.

4 mini muffins: 234 cal., 10g fat (3g sat. fat), 45mg chol., 560mg sod., 26g carb. (9g sugars, 1g fiber), 10g pro.
Diabetic exchanges: 1½ starch, 1 medium-fat meat, ½ fat.

EASY BREAKFAST STRATA

We put together this hearty breakfast casserole and pop it in the fridge the night before. That way, we don't have to deal with prep work and dirty dishes first thing in the morning. We just bake and enjoy!
—*Debbie Johnson, Centertown, MO*

....

PREP: 25 min. + chilling • **BAKE:** 30 min. • **MAKES:** 12 servings

1 loaf (1 lb.) herb or cheese bakery bread, cubed
1 lb. bulk pork sausage
1 medium green pepper, chopped
1 medium onion, chopped
1 cup shredded cheddar cheese
6 large eggs
1 tsp. ground mustard
2 cups 2% milk

1. Place bread cubes in a greased 13x9-in. baking dish. In a large skillet, cook and crumble sausage with pepper and onion over medium-high heat until no longer pink, 5-7 minutes. With a slotted spoon, place the sausage mixture over bread. Sprinkle with cheese.

2. In a large bowl, whisk together eggs, mustard and milk; pour over top. Refrigerate, covered, overnight.

3. Preheat oven to 350°. Remove strata from refrigerator while oven heats.

4. Bake, uncovered, until a knife inserted in the center comes out clean, 30-35 minutes. Let stand 5 minutes before cutting.

Freeze option: Cover and freeze the unbaked casserole. To use, partially thaw in refrigerator overnight. Remove from refrigerator 30 minutes before baking. Preheat oven to 350°. Bake the casserole as directed, increasing time as necessary to heat through and for a thermometer inserted in the center to read 165°.

1 piece: 295 cal., 16g fat (6g sat. fat), 126mg chol., 555mg sod., 23g carb. (4g sugars, 2g fiber), 14g pro.

BREAKFAST BURRITO CASSEROLE

A friend gave me her burrito casserole recipe, and I tweaked it a bit to fit my family.
I love to refrigerate this zippy breakfast overnight so it's ready for the oven in the morning.
—Krista Yoder, Abbeville, SC

PREP: 25 min. • **BAKE:** 30 min. • **MAKES:** 8 servings

8   large eggs
⅓   cup 2% milk
½   tsp. salt
½   tsp. pepper
1   lb. bulk pork sausage
1   cup sour cream
1   can (10¾ oz.) condensed
    cream of chicken soup,
    undiluted
4   flour tortillas (10 in.),
    cut into 1-in. pieces
1⅓ cups salsa, divided
⅔   cup shredded
    cheddar cheese
⅔   cup shredded part-skim
    mozzarella cheese
    Optional: Enchilada sauce
    and thinly sliced
    green onions

1. Preheat oven to 350°. Whisk together eggs, milk, salt and pepper. In a large skillet coated with cooking spray, cook and stir egg mixture over medium heat until thickened and no liquid egg remains; remove.

2. In the same skillet, cook and crumble sausage over medium heat until no longer pink, 5-7 minutes; drain. Stir together the sour cream and soup. Spread half the sour cream mixture in an ungreased 13x9-in. baking dish. Layer with half the tortilla pieces, half the salsa, the scrambled eggs, the sausage, and the remaining tortillas and sour cream mixture. Top with the remaining salsa; sprinkle with cheeses.

3. Bake, uncovered, until heated through, 30-35 minutes. If desired, serve with enchilada sauce and green onions.

To make ahead: Refrigerate unbaked casserole, covered, several hours or overnight. To use, preheat oven to 350°. Remove casserole from refrigerator while oven heats. Bake as directed, increasing time by 5 minutes.

1 cup: 506 cal., 34g fat (14g sat. fat), 243mg chol., 1419mg sod., 27g carb. (5g sugars, 2g fiber), 22g pro.

SHEET-PAN BACON & EGGS BREAKFAST

I re-created this recipe from an inspiring post I saw on social media. The result was a hit! Feel free to experiment—for example, you could try different cheeses, change up the spices or use seasoned potatoes.
—*Bonnie Hawkins, Elkhorn, WI*

PREP: 20 min. • **BAKE:** 40 min. • **MAKES:** 8 servings

10 bacon strips
1 pkg. (30 oz.) frozen shredded hash brown potatoes, thawed
1 tsp. garlic powder
1 tsp. dried basil
1 tsp. dried oregano
½ tsp. salt
½ tsp. crushed red pepper flakes
1½ cups shredded pepper jack cheese
1 cup shredded cheddar cheese
8 large eggs
¼ tsp. pepper
¼ cup chopped green onions

1. Preheat oven to 400°. Place the bacon in a single layer in a 15x10x1-in. baking sheet. Bake until partially cooked but not crisp, about 10 minutes. Remove to paper towels to drain; leave drippings in the pan. When cool enough to handle, chop bacon; set aside.

2. In a large bowl, combine potatoes and garlic powder, basil, oregano, salt and red pepper flakes; spread evenly into the drippings in the pan. Bake until golden brown, 25-30 minutes.

3. Sprinkle with cheeses. With the back of a spoon, make 8 wells in the potato mixture. Break an egg into each well; sprinkle with pepper and reserved bacon. Bake until egg whites are completely set and yolks begin to thicken but are not hard, 12-14 minutes. Sprinkle with green onions.

1 serving: 446 cal., 30g fat (13g sat. fat), 246mg chol., 695mg sod., 22g carb. (2g sugars, 1g fiber), 22g pro.

MINI HAM & CHEESE QUICHES

For a yummy breakfast or brunch, we bake miniature quiches loaded with ham and cheddar in muffin pans. Salad croutons eliminate the need for a crust!
—*Lois Enger, Colorado Springs, CO*

TAKES: 30 min. • **MAKES:** 1 dozen

1 cup salad croutons
1 cup shredded
  cheddar cheese
1 cup chopped
  fully cooked ham
4 large eggs
1½ cups 2% milk
1½ tsp. dried parsley flakes
½ tsp. Dijon mustard
¼ tsp. salt
⅛ tsp. onion powder
  Dash pepper

1. Preheat oven to 325°. Divide croutons, cheese and ham among 12 greased muffin cups. In a large bowl, whisk the remaining ingredients until blended. Divide egg mixture among prepared muffin cups.

2. Bake 15-20 minutes or until a knife inserted in the center comes out clean. Let stand 5 minutes before removing from pan. Serve warm.

1 mini quiche: 107 cal., 6g fat (3g sat. fat), 81mg chol., 328mg sod., 4g carb. (2g sugars, 0 fiber), 8g pro.

TEST KITCHEN TIP

Give these bites a taste of the Southwest by replacing the cheddar with a Mexican cheese blend and adding a few dashes of hot sauce to the whisked ingredients. Serve the zesty quiches with salsa on the side.

HOME-FOR-CHRISTMAS FRUIT BAKE

As this holiday favorite bakes, the cinnamony aroma that fills the house gets mouths watering in anticipation. The fruit comes out tender and slightly tart, while the pecan halves add a delightful crunch.
—*Bonnie Baumgardner, Sylva, NC*

PREP: 15 min. • **BAKE:** 45 min. • **MAKES:** 12 servings

1 medium apple,
   peeled and thinly sliced
1 tsp. lemon juice
1 can (20 oz.) pineapple
   chunks
1 can (29 oz.) peach halves,
   drained
1 can (29 oz.) pear halves,
   drained
1 jar (6 to 8 oz.) maraschino
   cherries
½ cup pecan halves
⅓ cup packed brown sugar
1 Tbsp. butter, melted
1 tsp. ground cinnamon

1. Preheat oven to 325°. Toss apple slices with lemon juice. Arrange in a greased 2½-qt. baking dish. Drain pineapple, reserving ¼ cup juice. Combine pineapple, peaches and pears; spoon over apples. Top with the cherries and pecans; set aside.

2. In a small saucepan, combine brown sugar, butter, cinnamon and reserved juice. Cook and stir over low heat until sugar is dissolved and butter is melted. Pour over fruit. Bake, uncovered, until the apples are tender, about 45 minutes. Serve warm.

¾ cup: 220 cal., 4g fat (1g sat. fat), 3mg chol., 21mg sod., 49g carb. (44g sugars, 3g fiber), 1g pro.

BACON & EGG LASAGNA

My sister-in-law served this special breakfast lasagna one year on Easter morning. Our whole family loved the combination of bacon, eggs, noodles and cheese.
—*Dianne Meyer, Graniteville, VT*

PREP: 45 min. • **BAKE:** 35 min. + standing • **MAKES:** 12 servings

1 lb. bacon strips, diced
1 large onion, chopped
⅓ cup all-purpose flour
½ to 1 tsp. salt
¼ tsp. pepper
4 cups 2% milk
12 lasagna noodles, cooked and drained
12 hard-boiled large eggs, sliced
2 cups shredded Swiss cheese
⅓ cup grated Parmesan cheese
2 Tbsp. minced fresh parsley, optional

1. In a large skillet, cook bacon until crisp. Remove with a slotted spoon to paper towels. Drain, reserving ⅓ cup drippings. In the drippings, saute onion until tender. Stir in the flour, salt and pepper until blended. Gradually stir in milk. Bring to a boil; cook and stir for 2 minutes or until thickened. Remove from the heat.

2. Spread ½ cup sauce in a greased 13x9-in. baking dish. Layer with 4 noodles and a third each of the eggs, bacon, Swiss cheese and remaining sauce. Repeat layers twice. Sprinkle with Parmesan cheese.

3. Bake, uncovered, at 350° until bubbly, 35-40 minutes. If desired, sprinkle with parsley. Let stand for 15 minutes before cutting.

1 piece: 386 cal., 20g fat (9g sat. fat), 252mg chol., 489mg sod., 28g carb. (7g sugars, 1g fiber), 23g pro.

SAUSAGE & CRESCENT ROLL CASSEROLE

When I had to make a dish for a baby shower, I tried this tasty casserole. It saved the day! The prep took just 15 minutes, giving me time to finish decorating for the party.
—Melody Craft, Conroe, TX

PREP: 15 min. • **BAKE:** 35 min. • **MAKES:** 12 servings

1   lb. bulk pork sausage
1   tube (8 oz.) refrigerated crescent rolls
2   cups shredded part-skim mozzarella cheese
8   large eggs
2   cups 2% milk
½   tsp. salt
¼   tsp. pepper

TEST KITCHEN TIP

Use spicy or mild Italian sausage in this recipe for a flavor twist.

1. Preheat oven to 375°. In a large skillet, cook sausage over medium heat 6-8 minutes or until no longer pink, breaking into crumbles; drain. Unroll crescent roll dough into a greased 13x9-in. baking dish. Seal the seams and perforations. Sprinkle with sausage and cheese.

2. In a large bowl, whisk eggs, milk, salt and pepper. Pour over sausage and cheese.

3. Bake, uncovered, 35-40 minutes or until a knife inserted in the center of the casserole comes out clean. Let stand 5-10 minutes before serving.

To make ahead: Refrigerate unbaked casserole, covered, several hours or overnight. To use, preheat oven to 375°. Remove casserole from refrigerator while oven heats. Bake as directed, increasing time as necessary until a knife inserted in the center comes out clean. Let stand 5-10 minutes before serving.

1 piece: 283 cal., 19g fat (6g sat. fat), 160mg chol., 662mg sod., 12g carb. (4g sugars, 0 fiber), 15g pro.

CHAPTER 3

CROWD-PLEASING SIDES & SALADS

These standout accompaniments—including cheesy pasta, slow-cooked beans and golden rolls—are bound to steal the show!

SLOW-COOKER POTLUCK BEANS

On the morning of our family potluck, I still hadn't figured out what I was going to bring.
I threw together this recipe while drinking my cup of coffee. By the end of the event,
the beans were all gone and someone had already washed my crock for me!
—Mary Anne Thygesen, Portland, OR

PREP: 10 min. • **COOK:** 4 hours • **MAKES:** 12 servings

1 cup brewed coffee
½ cup packed brown sugar
¼ cup spicy brown mustard
2 Tbsp. molasses
2 cans (16 oz. each) butter beans
2 cans (16 oz. each) kidney beans
2 cans (16 oz. each) navy beans

In a greased 3- or 4-qt. slow cooker, mix the first 4 ingredients. Rinse and drain the beans; stir into coffee mixture. Cook, covered, on low until flavors are blended, 4-5 hours.

Freeze option: Freeze the cooled beans in freezer containers. To use, partially thaw in the refrigerator overnight. Heat through in a covered saucepan, stirring occasionally; add water if necessary.

½ cup: 243 cal., 0 fat (0 sat. fat), 0 chol., 538mg sod., 50g carb. (13g sugars, 10g fiber), 14g pro.

TEST KITCHEN TIP

Add a tangy twist to this side by stirring a tablespoon of your favorite barbecue sauce into the cooked beans before serving.

POTLUCK PAN ROLLS

The made-from-scratch flavor of these soft, light rolls just can't be beat.
Folks have come to expect me to bring them to potlucks—and are disappointed if I don't!
—Carol Mead, Los Alamos, NM

PREP: 20 min. + rising • **BAKE:** 20 min. • **MAKES:** 27 rolls

1 pkg. (¼ oz.) active dry yeast
⅓ cup plus 1 tsp. sugar, divided
1½ cups warm water (110° to 115°), divided
½ cup butter, melted
2 large eggs
¼ cup instant nonfat dry milk powder
1¼ tsp. salt
5½ to 6 cups all-purpose flour

1. In a large bowl, dissolve yeast and 1 tsp. sugar in ½ cup water. Add the butter, eggs, dry milk powder, salt, 3 cups flour, and the remaining sugar and water. Beat on medium speed for 3 minutes. Stir in enough remaining flour to form a soft dough.

2. Turn dough onto a floured surface; knead until smooth and elastic, about 6-8 minutes. Place in a greased bowl, turning once to grease top. Cover and let rise in a warm place until doubled, about 1½ hours.

3. Punch dough down. Divide into 27 pieces; shape into balls. Place 18 balls in a greased 13x9-in. baking pan and remaining balls in a greased 9-in. square baking pan. Cover and let rise until doubled, about 45 minutes.

4. Bake at 375° for 17-20 minutes or until golden brown. Cool on wire racks.

1 roll: 141 cal., 4g fat (1g sat. fat), 14mg chol., 158mg sod., 23g carb. (3g sugars, 1g fiber), 3g pro.

LAYERED GARDEN BEAN SALAD

For easy entertaining, assemble this a few hours before guests arrive, then cover and refrigerate it until serving time. Tossing in some sliced rotisserie chicken, salmon or tuna turns the salad into a light lunch entree.
—*Melissa Wharton, Cincinnati, OH*

TAKES: 20 min. • **MAKES:** 16 servings

- 2 cups shredded romaine
- 2 cans (15 oz. each) black beans, rinsed and drained
- 2 Tbsp. chopped red onion
- 2 cups frozen corn, thawed
- 2 English cucumbers, chopped
- 4 medium tomatoes, chopped
- ½ cup reduced-fat ranch salad dressing
- 1 tsp. cumin seeds

In a 4-qt. glass bowl, layer the first 6 ingredients. In a small bowl, mix salad dressing and cumin seeds; drizzle over salad.

1 cup: 93 cal., 2g fat (0 sat. fat), 2mg chol., 180mg sod., 15g carb. (3g sugars, 4g fiber), 4g pro. **Diabetic exchanges:** 1 starch.

TEST KITCHEN TIP

Change the flavors of this salad by using different beans and choosing a complementary dressing. For example, try chickpeas with a Greek-style dressing or kidney beans with a bacon-flavored ranch.

CHEESY SCALLOPED POTATOES & HAM

This satisfying dish is the definition of comfort food—hearty, rich and creamy.
The recipe makes two 13x9-inch casseroles, so it's fantastic for a crowd.
—*Salina Bontrager, Kalona, IA*

PREP: 45 min. • **BAKE:** 1¾ hours • **MAKES:** 2 casseroles (8 servings each)

2 cans (10¾ oz. each) condensed cream of chicken soup, undiluted
2 cups sour cream
⅔ cup butter, melted
1 tsp. garlic powder
1 tsp. pepper
6½ lbs. potatoes, peeled and cut into ¼-in. slices
6 cups cubed fully cooked ham (about 2½ lbs.)
1 pkg. (16 oz.) Velveeta, cubed

1. Preheat oven to 350°. Mix the first 5 ingredients. Stir in the potatoes, ham and cheese. Transfer to 2 greased 13x9-in. baking dishes.

2. Bake, covered, 1 hour. Uncover and bake until the potatoes are tender, 45-55 minutes longer.

Freeze option: Cover and freeze the unbaked casseroles. To use, partially thaw in refrigerator overnight. Remove from refrigerator 30 minutes before baking. Preheat oven to 350°. Bake casseroles as directed, increasing the time as necessary to heat through and for a thermometer inserted in center to read 165°.

1½ cups: 491 cal., 28g fat (15g sat. fat), 106mg chol., 1664mg sod., 34g carb. (5g sugars, 2g fiber), 23g pro.

SLOW-COOKER CITRUS CARROTS

My mom tweaked a carrot recipe to suit her tastes, and the result was so delicious.
Feel free to do the cooking a day ahead of time, store your side dish
in the refrigerator and reheat before the party.
—*Julie Puderbaugh, Berwick, PA*

PREP: 10 min. • **COOK:** 4¼ hours • **MAKES:** 12 servings

12 cups frozen sliced carrots (about 48 oz.), thawed
1¾ cups orange juice
½ cup sugar
3 Tbsp. butter, cubed
½ tsp. salt
3 Tbsp. cornstarch
¼ cup cold water
Minced fresh parsley, optional

1. In a 3- or 4-qt. slow cooker, combine the first 5 ingredients. Cook, covered, on low 4-5 hours or until carrots are tender.

2. In a small bowl, mix cornstarch and cold water until smooth; gradually stir into slow cooker. Cook, covered, on high until sauce is thickened, 15-30 minutes. Garnish with fresh parsley if desired.

¾ cup: 136 cal., 4g fat (2g sat. fat), 8mg chol., 208mg sod., 25g carb. (18g sugars, 5g fiber), 1g pro.

POTLUCK MACARONI & CHEESE

You'll always have a winner at the potluck when you bring macaroni and cheese. Here's an extra-rich, creamy version for the slow cooker.
—*Jennifer Babcock, Chicopee, MA*

PREP: 25 min. • **COOK:** 2 hours • **MAKES:** 16 servings

3 cups uncooked elbow macaroni
1 pkg. (16 oz.) Velveeta, cubed
2 cups shredded Mexican cheese blend
2 cups shredded white cheddar cheese
1¾ cups whole milk
1 can (12 oz.) evaporated milk
¾ cup butter, melted
3 large eggs, lightly beaten

1. Cook macaroni according to package directions for al dente; drain. Transfer to a greased 5-qt. slow cooker. Stir in remaining ingredients.

2. Cook, covered, on low 2-2½ hours or until a thermometer reads at least 160°, stirring once.

¾ cup: 388 cal., 28g fat (17g sat. fat), 122mg chol., 652mg sod., 16g carb. (6g sugars, 0 fiber), 17g pro.

TEST KITCHEN TIP

Dress up this decadent dish with a sprinkling of finely chopped fresh parsley or even a few dashes of paprika or chili powder.

SPICED APPLESAUCE

Cardamom and mace add some delightfully different spices to this homemade applesauce. It's a special way to enjoy autumn's apple harvest.
—*Janet Thomas, McKees Rocks, PA*

PREP: 20 min. • **COOK:** 30 min. • **MAKES:** 9 cups

6 lbs. tart apples (about 18 medium), peeled and quartered
1 cup apple cider or juice
¾ cup sugar
2 Tbsp. lemon juice
1 cinnamon stick (3 in.)
1 tsp. ground ginger
1 tsp. vanilla extract
½ tsp. ground nutmeg
½ tsp. ground mace
¼ to ½ tsp. ground cardamom

Place all ingredients in a Dutch oven. Cover and cook over medium-low heat for 30-40 minutes or until apples are tender, stirring occasionally. Remove from heat; discard cinnamon stick. Mash the apples to desired consistency. Serve warm or cold. Store in the refrigerator.

½ cup: 113 cal., 0 fat (0 sat. fat), 0 chol., 2mg sod., 29g carb. (0 sugars, 2g fiber), 0 pro. **Diabetic exchanges:** 2 fruit.

SOFT ONION BREADSTICKS

Store-bought dough just can't compare to breads made from scratch. These breadsticks bake up golden and chewy to perfectly complement pastas, soups and more.
—*Maryellen Hays, Wolcottville, IN*

....

PREP: 30 min. + rising • **BAKE:** 20 min. • **MAKES:** 2 dozen

¾ cup chopped onion
1 Tbsp. canola oil
1 pkg. (¼ oz.) active dry yeast
½ cup warm water (110° to 115°)
½ cup warm 2% milk (110° to 115°)
¼ cup butter, softened
2 large eggs, room temperature, divided use
1 Tbsp. sugar
1½ tsp. salt
3½ to 4 cups all-purpose flour
2 Tbsp. cold water
2 Tbsp. sesame seeds
1 Tbsp. poppy seeds

1. In a small skillet, saute onion in oil until tender; cool. In a large bowl, dissolve yeast in warm water. Add the milk, butter, 1 egg, sugar, salt and 1 cup flour. Beat on medium speed for 2 minutes. Stir in onion and enough remaining flour to form a soft dough.

2. Turn onto a floured surface; knead until smooth and elastic, 6-8 minutes. Place in a greased bowl, turning once to grease top. Cover and let rise in a warm place until doubled, about 1 hour.

3. Punch the dough down. Let stand for 10 minutes. Turn onto a lightly floured surface; divide into 32 pieces. Shape each piece into an 8-in. rope. Place 2 in. apart on greased baking sheets. Cover and let rise for 15 minutes.

4. Beat cold water and remaining egg; brush over the breadsticks. Sprinkle half with sesame seeds and half with poppy seeds. Bake at 350° for 16-22 minutes or until golden brown. Remove to wire racks.

1 breadstick: 82 cal., 3g fat (1g sat. fat), 16mg chol., 129mg sod., 12g carb. (1g sugars, 1g fiber), 2g pro.

7-LAYER GELATIN SALAD

My mother serves this showstopper for Christmas dinner every year. Use any gelatin flavors you like to create special color combinations for particular holidays or events.
—*Jan Hemness, Stockton, MO*

PREP: 30 min. + chilling • **MAKES:** 20 servings

4½ cups boiling water, divided
7 pkg. (3 oz. each) assorted flavored gelatin
4½ cups cold water, divided
1 can (12 oz.) evaporated milk, divided
1 carton (8 oz.) frozen whipped topping, thawed
Optional: Sliced strawberries and kiwifruit

1. In a small bowl, add ¾ cup boiling water to 1 gelatin package; stir 2 minutes to completely dissolve. Stir in ¾ cup cold water. Pour into a 3-qt. trifle or glass bowl. Refrigerate until set but not firm, about 40 minutes.

2. In a clean bowl, dissolve another gelatin package into ½ cup boiling water. Stir in ½ cup cold water and ½ cup milk. Spoon over the first layer. Refrigerate until set but not firm.

3. Repeat 5 times, alternating plain and creamy gelatin layers. Refrigerate each layer until set but not firm before adding the next layer. Refrigerate, covered, overnight. Serve with whipped topping and, if desired, fruit.

1 serving: 163 cal., 3g fat (3g sat. fat), 6mg chol., 85mg sod., 30g carb. (30g sugars, 0 fiber), 4g pro.

TEST KITCHEN TIP

If your event calls for serving on individual plates, make this recipe in a 13x9-in. dish coated with cooking spray instead, following the recipe as directed. Then cut the salad into squares to serve and show off the layers!

WHEELY-GOOD PASTA SALAD

Who can resist fun wagon wheel pasta? Combine it with just five other ingredients for a yummy salad that's ready in less than half an hour.
—*Amber Kimmich, Powhatan, VA*

TAKES: 25 min. • **MAKES:** 12 servings

1 pkg. (16 oz.) wagon wheel pasta
8 oz. cheddar cheese, cut into small cubes
1 medium sweet red pepper, diced
1 can (3.8 oz.) sliced ripe olives, drained
2 tsp. minced fresh oregano
1 bottle (16 oz.) creamy Parmesan Romano salad dressing

Cook pasta according to package directions; drain and rinse in cold water. In a large serving bowl, combine pasta, cheddar cheese, red pepper, olives and oregano. Drizzle with the dressing and toss to coat. Cover and refrigerate until serving.

¾ cup: 414 cal., 26g fat (8g sat. fat), 27mg chol., 571mg sod., 32g carb. (5g sugars, 2g fiber), 11g pro.

READER RAVE

"I'm not a big fan of ripe olives, but I put them in anyway as the recipe directed—and they worked! I also used a Parmesan-pepper dressing, and it was tasty."
—PAUL111, TASTEOFHOME.COM

SLOW-COOKER CREAMED CORN

I'm a teacher, and this easy side is one of my go-to recipes for faculty potlucks. With just a little bite from the green chiles, this creamy corn is terrific for holidays, too.
—*Shelby Winters, Bonner Springs, KS*

PREP: 15 min. • **COOK:** 3 hours • **MAKES:** 8 servings

½ cup butter, cubed
1 medium onion, finely chopped
¼ cup finely chopped sweet red pepper
6 cups frozen corn (about 30 oz.), thawed
1 pkg. (8 oz.) cream cheese, cubed
1 can (4 oz.) chopped green chiles
1 tsp. salt
½ tsp. garlic powder
¼ tsp. pepper

In a large skillet, heat butter over medium-high heat. Add onion and red pepper; cook and stir 3-4 minutes or until tender. Transfer to a greased 3-qt. slow cooker. Stir in the remaining ingredients. Cook, covered, on low 3-4 hours or until heated through. Stir just before serving.

⅔ cup: 302 cal, 22g fat (13g sat. fat), 59mg chol., 536mg sod., 25g carb. (4g sugars, 3g fiber), 5g pro.

READER RAVE

"Wonderful side dish! It is easy to put together, has an amazing taste and goes great with roast. I will be making this a lot, as it's now a must-have in my family."
—DICENTRA01, TASTEOFHOME.COM

CONNIE'S TORTELLINI SALAD

Toss satisfying cheese tortellini and mozzarella with refreshing veggies for a substantial potluck salad. Sometimes I keep a bowl of this in the fridge for family members to dig into when they need something fast.
—*Connie Eaton, Pittsburgh, PA*

....

TAKES: 30 min. • **MAKES:** 16 servings

1 pkg. (13 oz.) dried cheese tortellini

1 medium zucchini, halved and sliced

1 cup Italian salad dressing

1 pint grape tomatoes

1 can (14 oz.) water-packed artichoke hearts, rinsed, drained and quartered

1 jar (11.1 oz.) pitted Greek olives, drained

1 carton (8 oz.) miniature fresh mozzarella cheese balls, drained

In a large saucepan, cook tortellini according to package directions. Drain; transfer to a large bowl. Immediately add zucchini and Italian dressing; toss to coat. Stir in the remaining ingredients. Serve warm or refrigerate and serve cold.

¾ cup: 260 cal., 17g fat (5g sat. fat), 28mg chol., 856mg sod., 19g carb. (2g sugars, 2g fiber), 7g pro.

CRUNCHY WHITE BAKED MACARONI & CHEESE

Creamy, cheesy and bubbly, this indulgent dish is comfort food at its best.
The topping of panko bread crumbs adds a pleasant bit of crunch.
—*Nicole Duffy, New Haven, CT*

PREP: 25 min. • **BAKE:** 30 min. + standing. • **MAKES:** 8 servings

1   pkg. (16 oz.) uncooked elbow macaroni

1   can (12 oz.) evaporated milk

1   cup whole milk

1   lb. white deli cheese, cubed

8   oz. cubed white cheddar cheese

1½ cups panko bread crumbs

½   cup grated Parmesan cheese

½   tsp. dried parsley flakes

1. In a large saucepan, cook macaroni according to package directions. Drain and set aside.

2. In same saucepan, combine the evaporated milk, whole milk, deli cheese and cheddar cheese. Cook and stir until the cheeses are melted and mixture is smooth. Stir in macaroni; heat through. Transfer to a greased 13x9-in. baking dish.

3. Combine panko bread crumbs, Parmesan and parsley flakes; sprinkle over the macaroni mixture. Cover and bake at 350° for 20 minutes. Uncover; bake until bubbly and golden brown, 10-15 minutes longer. Let stand for 10 minutes before serving.

1 cup: 639 cal., 31g fat (18g sat. fat), 104mg chol., 1091mg sod., 61g carb. (11g sugars, 2g fiber), 30g pro.

TZATZIKI POTATO SALAD

My son has an egg allergy, so this egg-free potato salad is perfect for him. It's popular with everyone else, too! For extra color, try adding radishes, apple and garlic dill pickles.
—*Cindy Romberg, Mississauga, ON*

. . . .

PREP: 25 min. + chilling • **MAKES:** 12 servings

- 3 lbs. small red potatoes, halved
- 1 carton (12 oz.) refrigerated tzatziki sauce
- 2 celery ribs, thinly sliced
- ½ cup plain Greek yogurt
- 2 green onions, chopped
- 2 Tbsp. snipped fresh dill
- 2 Tbsp. minced fresh parsley
- ½ tsp. salt
- ¼ tsp. celery salt
- ¼ tsp. pepper
- 1 Tbsp. minced fresh mint, optional

1. Place potatoes in a Dutch oven; add water to cover. Bring to a boil. Reduce heat; cook, uncovered, until tender, 10-15 minutes. Drain; cool completely.

2. In a small bowl, mix tzatziki sauce, celery, yogurt, green onions, dill, parsley, salt, celery salt, pepper and, if desired, mint. Spoon over potatoes; toss to coat. Refrigerate, covered, until cold.

¾ cup: 128 cal., 3g fat (2g sat. fat), 7mg chol., 190mg sod., 21g carb. (3g sugars, 2g fiber), 4g pro. **Diabetic exchanges:** 1½ starch, ½ fat.

FRUIT WITH POPPY SEED DRESSING

The tangy homemade dressing lends an extra-special touch to this refreshing fruit bowl. It's cool, colorful and so easy to prepare for an event.
—Peggy Mills, Texarkana, AR

PREP: 20 min. + standing • **MAKES:** 12 servings

3 Tbsp. honey
1 Tbsp. white vinegar
1 tsp. ground mustard
¼ tsp. salt
¼ tsp. onion powder
⅓ cup canola oil
1 tsp. poppy seeds
1 fresh pineapple, cut into 1½-in. cubes
3 medium kiwifruit, halved and sliced
2 cups fresh strawberries, halved

1. In a small bowl, whisk the first 5 ingredients. Gradually whisk in oil until blended. Stir in poppy seeds; let stand 1 hour.

2. In a large bowl, combine fruits. Drizzle with dressing; toss gently to coat.

1 cup: 129 cal., 7g fat (0 sat. fat), 0 chol., 51mg sod., 19g carb. (14g sugars, 2g fiber), 1g pro. **Diabetic exchanges:** 1½ fat, 1 fruit.

TEST KITCHEN TIP

Sliced bananas make a wonderful addition to this fruit salad. For best results, toss them in just before serving.

CONFETTI MACARONI SALAD

Bits of bright red and green veggies give a fun "confetti" look to my simple salad. The inspiration came from a recipe I found in a church cookbook when I was a young writer responsible for a newspaper's food section.

—Renee Page, Rochelle, IL

PREP: 20 min. + chilling • **MAKES:** 16 servings

1   pkg. (16 oz.) uncooked elbow macaroni
1½ cups mayonnaise
3   Tbsp. cider vinegar
1   Tbsp. prepared mustard
1½ tsp. salt
¼   tsp. pepper
1   medium sweet red pepper, chopped
1   celery rib, chopped
4   green onions, chopped
1   jar (4 oz.) diced pimientos, drained
¾   tsp. poppy seeds

1. Cook macaroni according to package directions; drain. Rinse with cold water and drain well.

2. In a large bowl, combine mayonnaise, cider vinegar, mustard, salt and pepper. Add macaroni and remaining ingredients; toss to coat. Refrigerate, covered, 2 hours or until cold.

¾ cup: 243 cal., 16g fat (2g sat. fat), 2mg chol., 342mg sod., 22g carb. (2g sugars, 1g fiber), 4g pro.

TEST KITCHEN TIP

This makes a versatile base recipe for just about any type of pasta salad you'd like to serve. Feel free to experiment with different mix-ins.

CALIFORNIA CITRUS & AVOCADO SALAD

This sunny green salad takes me back to my childhood in Southern California. My great-uncle had an orchard, and our family meals were filled with flavorful avocados, citrus fruits and nuts of all varieties.
—*Catherine Cassidy, Milwaukee, WI*

TAKES: 25 min. • **MAKES:** 12 servings

10 cups torn Bibb or Boston lettuce

1½ cups orange sections (about 2 medium oranges)

1 cup ruby red grapefruit sections (about 1 medium grapefruit)

2 medium ripe avocados, peeled and cubed

3 Tbsp. ruby red grapefruit juice

3 Tbsp. extra virgin olive oil

2 tsp. honey

½ tsp. salt

¾ cup crumbled queso fresco or feta cheese

¼ cup pistachios, chopped

Place the lettuce, oranges, grapefruit and avocados in a large bowl. In a small bowl, whisk grapefruit juice, oil, honey and salt until blended. Drizzle over the salad and toss gently to coat. Sprinkle with cheese and pistachios. Serve immediately.

1 cup: 132 cal., 9g fat (2g sat. fat), 5mg chol., 134mg sod., 10g carb. (5g sugars, 3g fiber), 4g pro. **Diabetic exchanges:** 2 fat, 1 vegetable.

POTLUCK GERMAN POTATO SALAD

I love bringing this classic dish to church potlucks because it's always a big hit. One attendee says he comes only so he can eat my potato salad!
—*Kathleen Rabe, Kiel, WI*

PREP: 20 min. • **COOK:** 25 min. • **MAKES:** 12 servings

- 3 lbs. small Yukon Gold potatoes, unpeeled (about 10)
- 2 celery ribs, chopped
- 1 small onion, chopped
- 1 cup water
- ½ cup white vinegar
- ¾ cup sugar
- 1 Tbsp. cornstarch
- ¼ tsp. salt
- ¼ tsp. pepper
- ½ lb. bacon strips, cooked and crumbled

1. Place potatoes in a large saucepan; add water to cover. Bring to a boil. Reduce heat; simmer, uncovered, just until tender, 12-15 minutes. Add the celery and onion; continue cooking until the vegetables are tender, about 5 minutes longer. Drain; set aside.

2. Meanwhile, in a small saucepan, whisk together next 6 ingredients. Bring to a boil; cook until thickened, about 2 minutes.

3. When cool enough to handle, slice potatoes; return to large saucepan with celery and onions. Add vinegar mixture, tossing to combine. Add bacon. Simmer mixture until heated through, 10-12 minutes. Serve warm.

⅔ cup: 194 cal., 3g fat (1g sat. fat), 7mg chol., 181mg sod., 39g carb. (15g sugars, 2g fiber), 5g pro.

CATALINA TACO SALAD

The teen campers at the youth camp my husband directs love this quick and easy taco salad. Our daughter has requested it two years in a row for her birthday dinner.
—*Kay Curtis, Guthrie, OK*

TAKES: 25 min. • **MAKES:** 12 servings

1½ lbs. lean ground beef (90% lean)
3 cups shredded cheddar cheese
1 can (15 oz.) pinto beans, rinsed and drained
2 medium tomatoes, seeded and chopped
1 large onion, chopped
1 bunch romaine, torn
1 pkg. (9¼ oz.) corn chips
1 bottle (24 oz.) Catalina salad dressing

1. In a large skillet, cook beef over medium heat until no longer pink; drain. Transfer to a large serving bowl.

2. Add the cheese, beans, tomatoes, onion, romaine and corn chips. Drizzle with dressing; gently toss to coat.

1 cup: 631 cal., 42g fat (12g sat. fat), 58mg chol., 1145mg sod., 39g carb. (16g sugars, 4g fiber), 21g pro.

SLOW-COOKER HOMEMADE
CHICKEN & RICE SOUP, 144

CHAPTER 4

MAKE & TAKE SLOW COOKER

Potlucks and slow cookers go hand in hand. This chapter lifts the lid on hot, hearty favorites you'll be proud to share.

....

MEDITERRANEAN SLOW-COOKER MASHED POTATOES

On Sundays I love to make my special turkey meat loaf. I get these delicious, fuss-free potatoes going ahead of time for the perfect side dish.
—*Kristen Heigl, Staten Island, NY*

PREP: 20 min. • **COOK:** 2 hours • **MAKES:** 10 servings

4 lbs. red potatoes, cubed
1 cup sour cream
½ cup butter, softened
3 garlic cloves, minced
2 Tbsp. snipped fresh dill
¾ tsp. salt
½ tsp. pepper
1 cup crumbled feta cheese

1. Place potatoes in a 6-qt. stockpot; add water to cover. Bring to a boil. Reduce heat; cook, uncovered, until tender, 10-15 minutes. Drain and coarsely mash.

2. Combine next 6 ingredients in a greased 5-qt. slow cooker; stir in the mashed potatoes and feta until well combined. Cook, covered, on low until heated through, 2-3 hours.

¾ cup: 287 cal., 15g fat (10g sat. fat), 46mg chol., 377mg sod., 30g carb. (3g sugars, 4g fiber), 6g pro.

TEST KITCHEN TIP

To make the best, fluffiest mashed potatoes, drain them well after boiling to prevent excess water from getting in the mix. Then mash them using a potato masher, ricer or fork. Resist the temptation to use a blender or food processor—they may be quick and convenient, but they'll also result in a gluey texture.

PINEAPPLE UPSIDE-DOWN DUMP CAKE

Whatever the season, this dump cake filled with pecans, cherries and pineapple is a winner. The recipe works well with gluten-free and sugar-free cake mixes, too.
—*Karin Gatewood, Dallas, TX*

PREP: 10 min. • **COOK:** 2 hours + standing • **MAKES:** 10 servings

¾ cup butter, divided
⅔ cup packed brown sugar
1 jar (6 oz.) maraschino cherries, drained
½ cup chopped pecans, toasted
1 can (20 oz.) unsweetened pineapple tidbits or crushed pineapple, undrained
1 pkg. yellow cake mix (regular size)
Vanilla ice cream, optional

1. In a microwave, melt ½ cup butter; stir in brown sugar. Spread evenly onto bottom of a greased 5-qt. slow cooker. Sprinkle with cherries and pecans; top with pineapple. Sprinkle evenly with dry cake mix. Melt remaining butter; drizzle over top.

2. Cook, covered, on high until fruit mixture is bubbly, about 2 hours. (To avoid scorching, rotate slow cooker insert one-half turn midway through cooking, lifting carefully with oven mitts.)

3. Turn off slow cooker; let stand, uncovered, 30 minutes before serving. If desired, serve with ice cream.

½ cup: 455 cal., 22g fat (10g sat. fat), 37mg chol., 418mg sod., 66g carb. (47g sugars, 1g fiber), 3g pro.

TEST KITCHEN TIP

In this recipe, the large slow cooker keeps the ingredient layers thin and promotes even cooking. When adding the cake mix, sprinkle it in an even layer. If it's piled high in the center, the middle of the cake may not cook completely. Be sure to let the cake stand, uncovered, after cooking to allow the steam to escape and the dessert to set up a bit.

CHICKEN CORDON BLEU SLIDERS

I'm a big fan of sandwiches and love coming up with my own creations. Inspired by the meat mixture in sloppy joes, I combined shredded chicken, cheese and chopped ham to make fun sliders.
—*Carolyn Eskew, Dayton, OH*

PREP: 20 min. • **COOK:** 2½ hours + standing • **MAKES:** 2 dozen

1½ lbs. boneless skinless chicken breasts
1 garlic clove, minced
¼ tsp. salt
¼ tsp. pepper
1 pkg. (8 oz.) cream cheese, cubed
2 cups shredded Swiss cheese
1¼ cups finely chopped fully cooked ham
2 pkg. (12 oz. each) Hawaiian sweet rolls, split
Chopped green onions

1. Place chicken in a greased 3-qt. slow cooker; sprinkle with garlic, salt and pepper. Top with cream cheese. Cook, covered, on low, 2½-3 hours or until a thermometer inserted in chicken reads 165°. Remove chicken; shred with 2 forks. Return to slow cooker.

2. Stir in Swiss cheese and ham. Cover and let stand 15 minutes or until cheese is melted. Stir before serving on rolls. Sprinkle with green onion.

1 slider: 209 cal., 10g fat (5g sat. fat), 53mg chol., 254mg sod., 17g carb. (6g sugars, 1g fiber), 14g pro.

WARM CIDER CRANBERRY PUNCH

I first prepared this at an instructional cooking camp. When I made some for my kids, they started requesting it every day! Enjoy the punch warm in winter...or cool it down and serve over ice for a tangy refresher in summer.
—Carol Gehringer, Raleigh, NC

PREP: 10 min. • **COOK:** 3 hours • **MAKES:** 20 servings

1 bottle (64 oz.) cranberry juice
6 cups apple cider or juice
2 cans (12 oz. each) frozen lemonade concentrate, thawed
1 medium lemon, cut into wedges
4 cinnamon sticks (3 in.)
2 tsp. whole cloves
1 tsp. whole allspice
Cranberries, lemon peel strips and additional cinnamon sticks, optional

In a 6-qt. slow cooker, combine cranberry juice, apple cider, lemonade concentrate and lemon. Place cinnamon sticks, cloves and allspice on a double thickness of cheesecloth. Gather corners of cheesecloth to enclose seasonings; tie securely with string. Place in slow cooker. Cook, covered, on low 3-4 hours or until heated through. Discard spice bag and lemon. If desired, garnish with cinnamon sticks, cranberries and lemon peel.

¾ cup: 83 cal., 0 fat (0 sat. fat), 0 chol., 10mg sod., 21g carb. (20g sugars, 0 fiber), 0 pro.

DID YOU KNOW?

You can cut strips of lemon peel for the garnish using a regular paring knife, but it's easier using a canelle, or channel knife. Many handheld citrus zesters come with a built-in canelle—it's that little V-shaped loop above the handle.

JALAPENO MAC & CHEESE

Years ago, a friend brought me a big mac-and-cheese casserole after I'd had surgery. She also shared the recipe, which I've enjoyed experimenting with ever since. Most recently, I added chopped jalapenos at the request of my son. What an awesome twist!
—*Teresa Gustafson, Elkton, MD*

PREP: 25 min. • **COOK:** 3 hours • **MAKES:** 15 servings

1 pkg. (16 oz.) uncooked elbow macaroni
6 Tbsp. butter, divided
4 jalapeno peppers, seeded and finely chopped
3 cups shredded cheddar cheese
2 cups shredded Colby-Monterey Jack cheese
2 cups whole milk
1 can (10¾ oz.) condensed cream of onion soup, undiluted
1 can (10¾ oz.) condensed cheddar cheese soup, undiluted
½ cup mayonnaise
¼ tsp. pepper
1 cup crushed Ritz crackers (about 25 crackers)

1. Cook macaroni according to package directions for al dente; drain. Transfer to a greased 5-qt. slow cooker.

2. Melt 2 Tbsp. butter in a large skillet over medium-high heat. Add jalapenos; cook and stir until crisp-tender, about 5 minutes. Add to slow cooker. Stir in the cheeses, milk, soups, mayonnaise and pepper.

3. Cook, covered, on low 3 hours or until cheese is melted and mixture is heated through. Melt remaining butter; stir in crackers. Sprinkle over macaroni mixture.

¾ cup: 428 cal., 27g fat (13g sat. fat), 53mg chol., 654mg sod., 33g carb. (5g sugars, 2g fiber), 14g pro.

TEST KITCHEN TIP

Be sure to cook the pasta just short of tender. It will continue to cook in the slow cooker.

SO-EASY STICKY CHICKEN WINGS

When my neighbor brought these tangy wings to a potluck, I just had to get the recipe.
I was thrilled to discover that they were not only delicious, but also super simple!
—*Jo Vanderwolf, Lillooet, BC*

PREP: 20 min. • **COOK:** 3 hours • **MAKES:** about 40 pieces

4 lbs. chicken wings
1 cup barbecue sauce
1 cup soy sauce
6 green onions, chopped, divided
1 Tbsp. sesame seeds

Using a sharp knife, cut through the 2 wing joints; discard the tips. Place the remaining wing pieces in a 4- or 5-qt. slow cooker. Stir in barbecue sauce, soy sauce and ¼ cup chopped green onions. Cook, covered, on high 3-4 hours or until tender. Sprinkle with sesame seeds and the remaining green onions.

1 piece: 68 cal., 4g fat (1g sat. fat), 14mg chol., 452mg sod., 3g carb. (2g sugars, 0 fiber), 6g pro.

DID YOU KNOW?

Sesame seeds are most commonly white, but you may also find light brown or black seeds. The black seeds have a stronger, nuttier flavor. All can be used interchangeably—the biggest difference is appearance.

WILD RICE WITH DRIED BLUEBERRIES

Our Thanksgiving dinner menu always includes this side dish. Sometimes I toss in toasted almonds; you could also add dried cherries or cranberries.
—*Janie Colle, Hutchinson, KS*

PREP: 15 min. • **COOK:** 3¼ hours • **MAKES:** 16 servings

2 Tbsp. butter
8 oz. sliced fresh mushrooms
3 cups uncooked wild rice
8 green onions, sliced
1 tsp. salt
½ tsp. pepper
4 cans (14½ oz. each) vegetable broth
1 cup chopped pecans, toasted
1 cup dried blueberries

In a large skillet, heat butter over medium heat. Add mushrooms; cook and stir 4-5 minutes or until tender. In a 5-qt. slow cooker, combine rice, mushrooms, onions, salt and pepper. Pour vegetable broth over rice mixture. Cook, covered, on low 3-4 hours or until rice is tender. Stir in pecans and berries. Cook, covered, 15 minutes longer or until heated through. If desired, top with additional sliced green onions.

¾ cup: 199 cal., 7g fat (1g sat. fat), 4mg chol., 163mg sod., 31g carb. (5g sugars, 4g fiber), 6g pro. **Diabetic exchanges:** 2 starch, 1½ fat.:

To toast nuts: Bake in a shallow pan in a 350° oven for 5-10 minutes or cook in a skillet over low heat until lightly browned, stirring occasionally.

TURKEY TACO MACARONI

Spice up macaroni and cheese with a taco twist featuring ground turkey instead of beef. When the mood strikes, we toss in chopped green peppers, too.
—*Barb Kondolf, Hamlin, NY*

PREP: 15 min. • **COOK:** 3 hours + standing • **MAKES:** 10 servings

2 Tbsp. canola oil, divided
4 cups uncooked elbow macaroni
2 lbs. ground turkey
1 medium onion, chopped
4 cans (8 oz. each) tomato sauce
1 cup water
1 cup salsa
1 envelope taco seasoning
2 cups shredded cheddar cheese

1. In a large skillet, heat 1 Tbsp. oil over medium heat. Add pasta; cook and stir 2-3 minutes or until pasta is toasted. Transfer to a 5-qt. slow cooker. In the same skillet, heat remaining oil over medium-high heat. Add ground turkey and onion; cook 6-8 minutes or until meat is no longer pink, breaking into crumbles.

2. Transfer to slow cooker. Stir in tomato sauce, water, salsa and taco seasoning. Cook, covered, 3-4 hours or until pasta is tender.

3. Remove insert; top with cheese. Let stand, covered, 15 minutes.

1 cup: 402 cal., 19g fat (6g sat. fat), 83mg chol., 1063mg sod., 32g carb. (4g sugars, 3g fiber), 29g pro.

SLOW-COOKER PIZZA DIP

For my daughter's pizza-themed birthday party, I came up with this chunky dip.
It was a hit! I've continued making it for potlucks and other events.
—*Stephanie Gates, Waterloo, IA*

PREP: 15 min. • **COOK:** 2 hours • **MAKES:** 20 servings

½ lb. ground beef
½ lb. bulk pork sausage
1 can (28 oz.) crushed tomatoes
½ cup diced green pepper
¼ cup grated Parmesan cheese
2 Tbsp. tomato paste
2 tsp. Italian seasoning
1 garlic clove, minced
¾ tsp. crushed red pepper flakes
¼ tsp. salt
¼ tsp. pepper
Hot garlic bread

1. In a large skillet, cook and crumble beef and sausage over medium heat until no longer pink, 5-7 minutes. Using a slotted spoon, transfer meat to a 3-qt. slow cooker. Stir in all remaining ingredients except bread.

2. Cook, covered, on low 2-3 hours or until heated through. Serve with bread.

Freeze option: Freeze the cooled dip in freezer containers. To use, partially thaw in the refrigerator overnight. Heat through in a saucepan, stirring occasionally.

¼ cup dip: 68 cal., 4g fat (1g sat. fat), 14mg chol., 198mg sod., 4g carb. (2g sugars, 1g fiber), 4g pro.

TEST KITCHEN TIP

One pound of Italian sausage may be substituted for the ½ pound ground beef and ½ pound pork sausage.

ROOT BEER BRATS

These soda-licious bratwursts are just as good served over rice as they are in buns.
Give the sauce even more flavor by adding a splash of root beer concentrate.
—*Pamela Thompson, Girard, IL*

PREP: 15 min. • **COOK:** 6 hours • **MAKES:** 10 servings

1 can (12 oz.) root beer
3 Tbsp. cornstarch
3 tsp. ground mustard
3 tsp. caraway seeds
10 uncooked bratwurst links
1 large onion, coarsely chopped
1 bottle (12 oz.) chili sauce
10 hoagie buns, toasted
Optional: Thinly sliced red onion and prepared mustard

1. Whisk the first 4 ingredients until blended. In a large nonstick skillet, brown bratwursts over medium-high heat. Transfer to a 4- or 5-qt. slow cooker. Add onion, chili sauce and root beer mixture.

2. Cook, covered, on low 6-8 hours or until a thermometer inserted in sausage reads at least 160°. Serve in buns. If desired, top with red onion and mustard.

1 serving: 563 cal., 30g fat (10g sat. fat), 63mg chol., 1575mg sod., 54g carb. (16g sugars, 2g fiber), 20g pro.

READER RAVE

"Wow, what great flavor! I used a Thai sweet chili sauce. Yes, you notice the heat a little—you won't doze off when eating this—but it's not overpowering at all. I added just a touch of mustard to the final brat and spooned a little of the sauce inside the bun before serving. I will make this recipe again without reservation."

—BILL GARRISON JR., TASTEOFHOME.COM

SLOW-COOKED HAM WITH PINEAPPLE SAUCE

In our house, this special main course is a must for holidays.
But the recipe is so easy to prepare, we indulge other times of year, too.
—*Terry Roberts, Yorktown, VA*

PREP: 10 min. • **COOK:** 6 hours • **MAKES:** 12 servings

1 fully cooked boneless ham (4 to 5 lbs.)
1 Tbsp. cornstarch
2 Tbsp. lemon juice
1 cup packed brown sugar
1 Tbsp. yellow mustard
¼ tsp. salt
1 can (20 oz.) unsweetened crushed pineapple, undrained

1. Place ham in a 5-qt. slow cooker. In a small saucepan, mix the cornstarch and lemon juice until smooth. Stir in the remaining ingredients; bring to a boil, stirring occasionally. Pour over ham, covering completely.

2. Cook, covered, on low 6-8 hours (a thermometer inserted in ham should read at least 140°).

4 oz. ham with ¼ cup sauce: 262 cal., 6g fat (2g sat. fat), 77mg chol., 1638mg sod., 27g carb. (25g sugars, 0 fiber), 28g pro.

Note: This recipe is not recommended for use with a spiral-sliced ham.

SLOW-COOKER TATER TOT CASSEROLE

What's better than classic Tater Tot casserole? One that's made in the slow cooker! You'll want to add this family-pleasing favorite to your regular rotation.
—*Nick Iverson, Denver, CO*

PREP: 25 min. • **COOK:** 6 hours + standing • **MAKES:** 12 servings

2 lbs. ground beef
1 large onion, chopped
1 lb. sliced fresh mushrooms
3 garlic cloves, minced
2 cans (10¾ oz. each) condensed cream of mushroom soup, undiluted
½ tsp. salt
½ tsp. pepper
1 lb. frozen cut green beans
1 bag (32 oz.) frozen Tater Tots
1 cup shredded cheddar cheese

1. In a large skillet, cook beef over medium-high heat until no longer pink, 5-6 minutes, breaking into crumbles; drain and transfer to a 5-qt. slow cooker. Add onions and mushrooms to skillet; cook over medium-high heat until vegetables are tender, 8-10 minutes. Add garlic; cook 1 minute longer. Stir in condensed soup, salt and pepper. Place vegetable mixture in slow cooker; add green beans and stir to combine. Top with Tater Tots and cheese.

2. Cook, covered, on low 6 hours. Let stand, uncovered, 15 minutes before serving.

1 serving: 383 cal., 22g fat (7g sat. fat), 58mg chol., 941mg sod., 27g carb. (3g sugars, 4g fiber), 20g pro.

TEST KITCHEN TIP

Give this family-friendly dish extra color by replacing the green beans with frozen mixed veggies.

SMOKY WHITE BEANS & HAM

Before meeting my husband here in Kentucky, I had never made or eaten this dish.
Now I serve it every week with a side of homemade sweet cornbread. Delicious!
—*Christine Duffy, Sturgis, KY*

PREP: 15 min. + soaking • **COOK:** 6 hours • **MAKES:** 10 servings

1 lb. dried great northern beans

3 smoked ham hocks (about 1½ lbs.)

1 large onion, chopped

3 cans (14½ oz. each) reduced-sodium chicken or beef broth

2 cups water

1 Tbsp. onion powder

1 Tbsp. garlic powder

2 tsp. pepper

Thinly sliced green onions, optional

1. Rinse and sort beans; soak according to package directions.

2. Drain and rinse beans, discarding the liquid. Transfer beans to a 6-qt. slow cooker. Add ham hocks. Stir in onion, broth, water and seasonings. Cook, covered, on low for 6-8 hours or until beans are tender.

3. Remove meat from bones when cool enough to handle; cut ham into small pieces and return to the slow cooker. Serve with a slotted spoon. Sprinkle with sliced green onions if desired.

⅔ cup: 195 cal., 2g fat (0 sat. fat), 8mg chol., 505mg sod., 32g carb. (2g sugars, 10g fiber), 15g pro. **Diabetic exchanges:** 2 starch, 2 lean meat.

READER RAVE

"I boiled the ham hocks first to remove a lot of the salt, and I used minced garlic instead of garlic powder. Other than that, I made the recipe as is. A great meal for the cold Canadian winters!"

—PAULETTE, TASTEOFHOME.COM

COUNTRY-STYLE BARBECUE RIBS

These get a good sear under the broiler, then become fall-apart tender in the slow cooker. Enjoy the ribs just as they are...or shred the meat to pile on buns for sandwiches.

—*Shannon Copley, Upper Arlington, OH*

PREP: 15 min. • **COOK:** 3 hours • **MAKES:** 10 servings

- 2 Tbsp. paprika
- 2 Tbsp. brown sugar
- 2 tsp. salt
- 2 tsp. garlic powder
- 2 tsp. chili powder
- 1 tsp. onion powder
- 1 tsp. ground chipotle pepper
- 1 tsp. pepper
- ¾ tsp. dried thyme
- 4 lbs. boneless country-style pork ribs
- 1 bottle (18 oz.) barbecue sauce
- ¾ cup amber beer or reduced-sodium chicken broth

1. Preheat broiler. Mix first 9 ingredients. Place pork in a foil-lined 15x10x1-in. pan; rub generously with seasonings. Broil 4-5 in. from heat until browned, 2-3 minutes per side.

2. Transfer to a 5-qt. slow cooker. Whisk together the barbecue sauce and beer; pour over ribs. Cook, covered, on low until tender, 3-4 hours.

3. Remove ribs. Reserve 2 cups cooking juices; discard remaining juices. Skim fat from reserved juices. Serve with ribs.

1 serving: 393 cal., 17g fat (6g sat. fat), 105mg chol., 1098mg sod., 26g carb. (20g sugars, 1g fiber), 33g pro.

TEST KITCHEN TIP

Country-style are the meatiest of all pork ribs. Look for highly marbled ribs; they might be labeled pork shoulder country-style ribs. Country-style ribs from the loin are leaner and won't be as tender and moist.

SMASHED SWEET POTATOES & APPLES

On Thanksgiving, oven space can be in short supply. So I decided to make part of our holiday dinner in the slow cooker. This not-too-sweet dish goes well with both turkey and ham.
—*Judy Batson, Tampa, FL*

PREP: 20 min. • **COOK:** 5 hours • **MAKES:** 10 servings

3 lbs. sweet potatoes, peeled and cubed (about 8 cups)

1½ lbs. tart apples, peeled and cubed (about 4 cups)

1½ cups unsweetened apple juice

1 bottle (12 oz.) light beer or additional unsweetened apple juice

1 cup packed brown sugar

1 cup sour cream

2 Tbsp. butter

Minced chives, optional

1. Place sweet potatoes and apples in a 6-qt. slow cooker. Add apple juice and beer. Cook, covered, on low 5-6 hours or until potatoes are tender.

2. Drain; return to slow cooker. Add brown sugar, sour cream and butter. Mash potato mixture to reach desired consistency. If desired, top with minced chives.

¾ cup: 338 cal., 7g fat (4g sat. fat), 12mg chol., 48mg sod., 67g carb. (45g sugars, 5g fiber), 3g pro.

Pressure cooker: Place sweet potatoes and apples in a 6-qt. electric pressure cooker; add apple juice and beer. Lock lid; close pressure-release valve. Adjust to pressure-cook on high for 12 minutes. Let pressure release naturally. Press cancel. Drain; return to pressure cooker. Add brown sugar, sour cream and butter. Mash potato mixture to reach desired consistency.

TRULY TASTY TURNIPS WITH GREENS

Every time I go to a church dinner with this savory dish, it's a hit.
Adjust the seasonings as you please to make this recipe your own.
—*Amy Inman, Hiddenite, NC*

PREP: 20 min. • **COOK:** 5 hours • **MAKES:** 14 servings

2¾ lbs. turnips, peeled and cut into ½-in. cubes

1 bunch fresh turnip greens (about 12 oz.), chopped

8 oz. cubed fully cooked country ham or 2 smoked ham hocks (about 1½ lbs.)

1 medium onion, chopped

3 Tbsp. sugar

1½ tsp. coarsely ground pepper

1¼ tsp. salt

2 cartons (32 oz. each) chicken broth

In a greased 6- or 7-qt. slow cooker, combine all the ingredients. Cook, covered, on low 5-6 hours or until vegetables are tender, stirring once. If using ham hocks, remove meat from bones when cool enough to handle; cut ham into small pieces and return to slow cooker. Serve with a slotted spoon.

¾ cup: 58 cal., 1g fat (0 sat. fat), 9mg chol., 514mg sod., 9g carb. (6g sugars, 2g fiber), 5g pro. **Diabetic exchanges:** 1 lean meat, 1 vegetable.

DID YOU KNOW?

Sugar is added to many recipes for turnip greens to offset their somewhat bitter flavor.

SLOW-COOKER HOMEMADE CHICKEN & RICE SOUP

I love making this from-scratch chicken soup loaded with rice and veggies.
The long cook time helps develop great homemade flavor.
—*Kevin Bruckerhoff, Columbia, MO*

PREP: 15 min. • **COOK:** 8 hours • **MAKES:** 4 qt.

3 qt. water
4 bone-in chicken breast halves (about 3 lbs.)
1½ tsp. salt
¼ tsp. pepper
¼ tsp. poultry seasoning
1 tsp. chicken bouillon granules
3 medium carrots, chopped
2 celery ribs, chopped
1 small onion, chopped
½ cup uncooked converted rice
Minced fresh parsley, optional

1. In a 6-qt. slow cooker, place the water, chicken, salt, pepper and poultry seasoning. Cover and cook on low 6-7 hours or until chicken is tender.

2. With a slotted spoon, remove chicken from broth. When cool enough to handle, remove meat from bones; discard skin and bones. Cut chicken into bite-sized pieces. Skim fat from broth; add chicken and next 5 ingredients. Cover and cook on high 1-2 hours or until vegetables and rice are tender. If desired, sprinkle with parsley.

1 cup: 202 cal., 6g fat (2g sat. fat), 66mg chol., 513mg sod., 10g carb. (1g sugars, 1g fiber), 25g pro.

SLOW-COOKED CHEESY CAULIFLOWER

After searching for a veggie recipe I could make in the slow cooker, I ended up creating my own creamy cauliflower dish with a bread crumb topping. We love it!
—Heather Corson, Casper, WY

PREP: 10 min. • **COOK:** 5 hours • **MAKES:** 16 servings

2 medium heads cauliflower, cut into florets (about 18 cups)
1 can (10¾ oz.) condensed cream of chicken soup, undiluted
2 cups shredded cheddar cheese
1 cup sour cream
½ tsp. salt
½ tsp. pepper
¼ cup butter, cubed
1 cup dry bread crumbs

1. In a 6-qt. slow cooker, combine cauliflower, soup and cheese. Cook, covered, on low for 5-6 hours or until cauliflower is tender. Stir in sour cream, salt and pepper.

2. In a small skillet, melt butter over medium heat. Add bread crumbs; cook and stir until golden brown, 2-3 minutes. Sprinkle over cauliflower.

¾ cup: 178 cal., 12g fat (7g sat. fat), 27mg chol., 411mg sod., 11g carb. (3g sugars, 2g fiber), 6g pro.

TEST KITCHEN TIP

To add another level of flavor to this dish, replace some of the cheddar cheese with Gruyere.

SLOW-COOKER CHEESEBURGER DIP

Craving a big, juicy cheeseburger? Enjoy one from the slow cooker! This fun appetizer requires less than 30 minutes of prep and uses ingredients I usually have on hand.
—*Cindi DeClue, Anchorage, AK*

PREP: 25 min. • **COOK:** 1¾ hours • **MAKES:** 16 servings

1 lb. lean ground beef (90% lean)
1 medium onion, chopped
1 pkg. (8 oz.) cream cheese, cubed
2 cups shredded cheddar cheese, divided
1 Tbsp. Worcestershire sauce
2 tsp. prepared mustard
¼ tsp. salt
⅛ tsp. pepper
1 medium tomato, chopped
¼ cup chopped dill pickles
Tortilla chips or crackers

1. In a large skillet, cook ground beef and onion over medium-high heat until beef is no longer pink and onion is tender, breaking up beef into crumbles, 6-8 minutes; drain. Transfer to a greased 1½- or 3-qt. slow cooker. Stir in the cream cheese, 1½ cups cheddar cheese, Worcestershire, mustard, salt and pepper. Sprinkle with remaining cheese.

2. Cook, covered, on low 1¾-2¼ hours or until mixture is heated through and cheese is melted. Top with tomatoes and pickles. Serve with tortilla chips.

¼ cup: 157 cal., 12g fat (6g sat. fat), 46mg chol., 225mg sod., 2g carb. (1g sugars, 0 fiber), 10g pro.

TEST KITCHEN TIP
Keep an eye on the dip toward the end of cooking. If the mixture cooks too long, the edges will get dark.

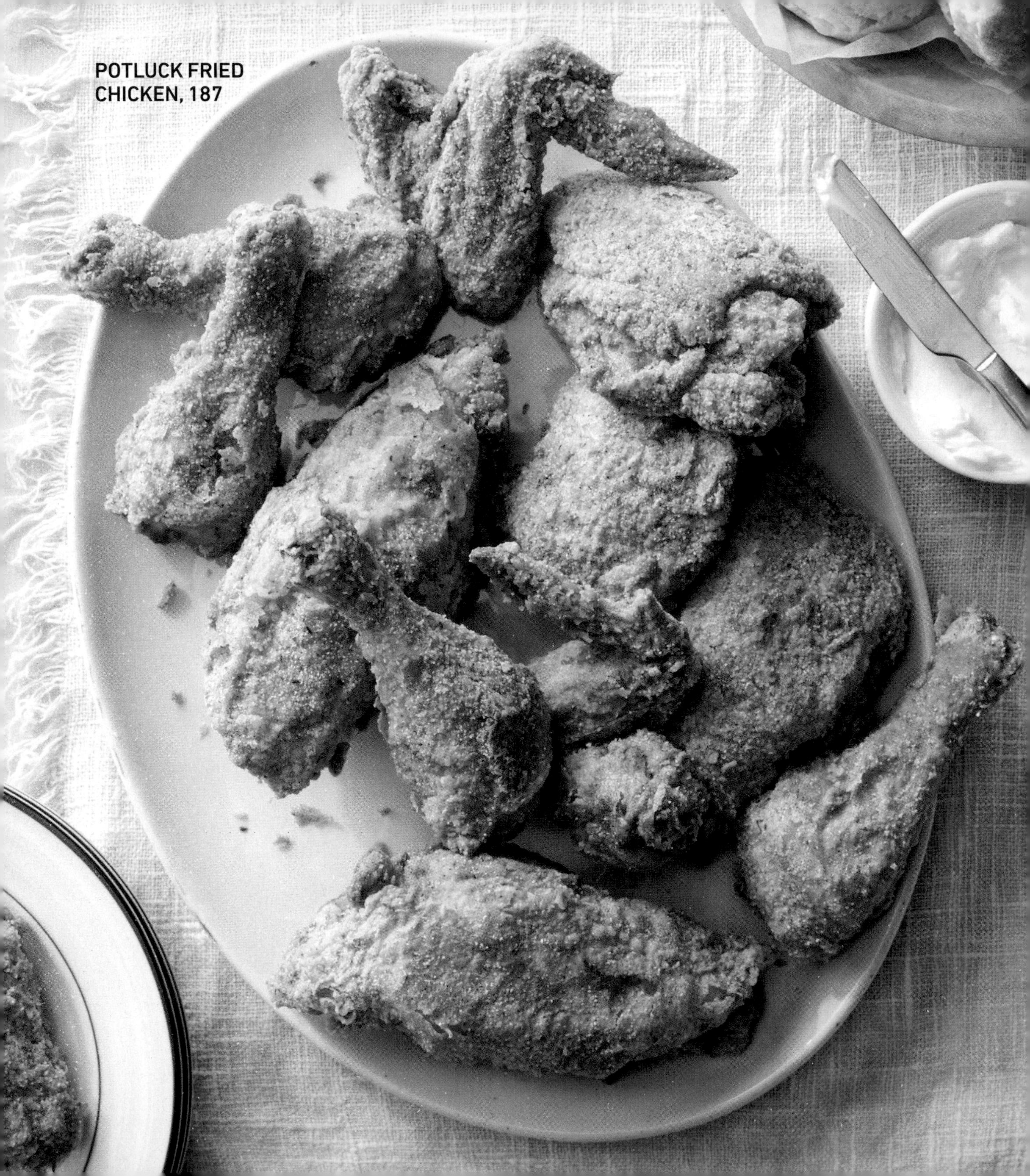

POTLUCK FRIED CHICKEN, 187

CHAPTER 5

ENTREES TO SHARE

Hungry crowds come running when you fill the buffet table with these tasty casseroles, sandwiches and other main dishes.

ABERDEEN BEEF PIE

As soon as it's set on the table, this hearty meat pie will be the center of attention.
The golden, flaky pastry crust tops a savory filling of tender beef and vegetables.
—*Peggy Goodrich, Enid, OK*

PREP: 1½ hours • **BAKE:** 35 min. + standing • **MAKES:** 12 servings

¼ lb. sliced bacon, diced
3 lbs. beef stew meat, cut into 1-in. cubes
1 cup chopped onion
1½ cups halved fresh baby carrots
6 Tbsp. all-purpose flour
1 cup beef broth
1 Tbsp. Worcestershire sauce
1 pkg. (10 oz.) frozen peas
½ tsp. salt
½ tsp. pepper
1 refrigerated pie crust
1 large egg, lightly beaten, optional

1. In a Dutch oven, cook bacon over medium heat until crisp. Remove to paper towels to drain. Brown the beef in drippings in batches; drain and set beef aside. Add onion to the pan; saute until crisp-tender. Add carrots, bacon and beef.

2. Meanwhile, in a small bowl, combine flour, broth and Worcestershire sauce until smooth; add to beef mixture. Bring to a boil. Reduce heat; cover and simmer until meat is tender, 1-1½ hours. Stir in peas, salt and pepper. Transfer to an ungreased 11x7-in. baking dish.

3. On a lightly floured surface, roll out pie crust into a 12x8-in. rectangle. Cut slits in pie crust. Place over the filling; trim and seal the edges. If desired, brush with beaten egg. Bake at 375° until crust is golden and filling is bubbly, 35-40 minutes. Let stand for 15 minutes before serving. Refrigerate leftovers.

1 serving: 308 cal., 14g fat (6g sat. fat), 76mg chol., 389mg sod., 18g carb. (3g sugars, 2g fiber), 25g pro.

BRATWURST SUPPER

This simple, homey dinner grills to perfection in foil packets. The chunks of bratwurst and veggies are easy to season with onion soup mix and a little soy sauce.
—*Janice Meyer, Medford, WI*

· ·

PREP: 10 min. • **GRILL:** 45 min. • **MAKES:** 12 servings

3 lbs. uncooked bratwurst links
3 lbs. small red potatoes, cut into wedges
1 lb. baby carrots
1 large red onion, sliced and separated into rings
2 jars (4½ oz. each) whole mushrooms, drained
¼ cup butter, cubed
1 envelope onion soup mix
2 Tbsp. soy sauce
½ tsp. pepper

1. For each of 2 foil packets, arrange a double thickness of heavy-duty foil (about 17x15 in.) on a flat surface.

2. Cut brats into thirds. Divide the brats, potatoes, carrots, onion and mushrooms evenly between the 2 double-layer foil rectangles. Dot with butter. Sprinkle with soup mix, soy sauce and pepper. Bring edges of foil together; crimp to seal, forming 2 large packets. Seal tightly; turn to coat.

3. Grill, covered, over medium heat for 23-28 minutes on each side or until the vegetables are tender and the sausage is no longer pink. Open foil carefully to allow steam to escape.

1 serving: 524 cal., 37g fat (14g sat. fat), 94mg chol., 1445mg sod., 28g carb. (4g sugars, 3g fiber), 19g pro.

GRILLED LEMON CHICKEN

My chicken gets a subtle but tangy twist from lemonade concentrate. With garlic, soy sauce and seasoned salt, the flavor keeps 'em coming back for more.
—Linda Nilsen, Anoka, MN

PREP: 5 min. • **GRILL:** 40 min. • **MAKES:** 12 servings

- ¾ cup thawed lemonade concentrate
- ⅓ cup soy sauce
- 1 garlic clove, minced
- 1 tsp. seasoned salt
- ½ tsp. celery salt
- ⅛ tsp. garlic powder
- 2 broiler/fryer chickens (3 to 3½ lbs. each), cut up

1. In a bowl, whisk the first 6 ingredients until combined. Pour half into a shallow glass dish. Cover and refrigerate remaining lemonade mixture.

2. Dip chicken into lemonade mixture, turning to coat; discard lemonade mixture. Grill chicken, covered, over medium heat for 30 minutes, turning occasionally. Brush with the reserved mixture. Grill 10-20 minutes longer, brushing frequently, until a thermometer reads 165°.

5 oz. cooked chicken: 320 cal., 17g fat (5g sat. fat), 104mg chol., 504mg sod., 6g carb. (5g sugars, 0 fiber), 34g pro.

READER RAVE

"I cut this recipe in half and used chunks of chicken breast. It was really good!"

—AHMOM, TASTEOFHOME.COM

TACO TWISTS

Why have tacos only in tortillas? For a fun change of pace, I bake the seasoned beef in crescent dough bundles. My family enjoys them as a hearty lunch or light dinner.

—*Carla Kreider, Quarryville, PA*

PREP: 15 min. • **BAKE:** 25 min. • **MAKES:** 12 servings

1 lb. ground beef
1 large onion, chopped
2 cups shredded cheddar cheese
1 cup salsa
1 can (4 oz.) chopped green chiles
1 tsp. garlic powder
½ tsp. hot pepper sauce
¼ tsp. salt
¼ tsp. ground cumin
3 tubes (8 oz. each) refrigerated crescent rolls
Optional: Shredded lettuce, sliced ripe olives, chopped tomatoes and sliced seeded jalapeno pepper

1. In a large skillet, cook beef and onion over medium heat until meat is no longer pink; drain. Stir in cheddar cheese, salsa, chiles, garlic powder, hot pepper sauce, salt and cumin.

2. Unroll the crescent roll dough and separate into 12 rectangles. Place on ungreased baking sheets; press perforations to seal. Place ½ cup meat mixture in the center of each rectangle. Bring 4 corners to the center and twist; pinch to seal.

3. Bake at 350° until golden brown, 25-30 minutes. Serve with toppings as desired.

Freeze option: Freeze baked, cooled taco twists for up to 3 months. Bake frozen twists on an ungreased baking sheet at 350° for until heated through, 20-25 minutes.

1 taco twist: 214 cal., 13g fat (7g sat. fat), 39mg chol., 463mg sod., 10g carb. (3g sugars, 1g fiber), 12g pro.

SOUTHWESTERN TURKEY BAKE

Getting my husband to eat veggies was a challenge—until I tried this casserole!
Creamy and cheesy with a kick from jalapenos, it's always satisfying.
—*Crystal Kolady, Henrietta, NY*

PREP: 20 min. • **BAKE:** 25 min. • **MAKES:** 12 servings

2 large onions, chopped
2 jalapeno peppers, seeded and chopped
2 Tbsp. butter
6 cups cubed cooked turkey
2 cans (10¾ oz. each) condensed cream of chicken soup, undiluted
2 cups sour cream
1 pkg. (10 oz.) frozen chopped spinach, thawed and squeezed dry
2 cups shredded Monterey Jack cheese
1 pkg. (9¾ oz.) nacho-flavored tortilla chips, crushed
4 green onions, sliced

1. Preheat oven to 350°. In a Dutch oven, saute onions and jalapenos in butter until tender. Stir in turkey, soup, sour cream and spinach. In a greased 13x9-in. baking dish, layer half the turkey mixture, cheese and tortilla chips. Repeat layers.

2. Bake, uncovered, until bubbly, 25-30 minutes.Let stand 5 minutes before serving. Sprinkle with sliced green onions.

1 piece: 464 cal., 28g fat (12g sat. fat), 106mg chol., 773mg sod., 23g carb. (3g sugars, 3g fiber), 30g pro.

READER RAVE

"I made this today for the second time. I used broccoli instead of spinach and prepared an extra casserole for a friend. She really liked it—and wanted the recipe! It's a real keeper for my family."

—REDCOW, TASTEOFHOME.COM

EASY & ELEGANT TENDERLOIN ROAST

I love the simplicity of this recipe. Just rub olive oil, garlic, salt and pepper over a tenderloin and pop it in the oven. In an hour or so, you'll have an impressive main dish for a crowd.
—*Mary Kandell, Huron, OH*

PREP: 10 min. • **BAKE:** 45 min. + standing • **MAKES:** 12 servings

1 beef tenderloin (5 lbs.)
2 Tbsp. olive oil
4 garlic cloves, minced
2 tsp. sea salt
1½ tsp. coarsely ground
    pepper

1. Preheat oven to 425°. Place the roast on a rack in a shallow roasting pan. In a small bowl, mix the oil, garlic, salt and pepper; rub over roast.

2. Roast until the meat reaches desired doneness (for medium-rare, a thermometer should read 135°; medium, 140°; medium-well, 145°), 45-65 minutes. Remove from oven; tent with foil. Let stand 15 minutes before slicing.

5 oz. cooked beef: 294 cal., 13g fat (5g sat. fat), 82mg chol., 394mg sod., 1g carb. (0 sugars, 0 fiber), 40g pro. **Diabetic exchanges:** 5 lean meat, ½ fat.

TEST KITCHEN TIP

For a simple shortcut, place 4 whole garlic cloves in your food processor and add the olive oil, sea salt and pepper. Then pulse a few times—it will combine the ingredients and mince the garlic at the same time.

BAKED HAM WITH HONEY-CHIPOTLE GLAZE

Easter events are even more special when you serve this sweet, smoky ham.
The recipe includes a delicious honey-orange variation, too.
—Taste of Home *Test Kitchen*

PREP: 10 min. • **BAKE:** 2 hours • **MAKES:** 16 servings

1 **fully cooked bone-in ham (8 to 10 lbs.)**
1 **cup packed brown sugar**
3 **Tbsp. honey**
2 **Tbsp. cider vinegar**
2¼ **cups ginger ale**
4 **chipotle peppers in adobo sauce, minced**
3 **garlic cloves, minced**
1½ **tsp. Dijon mustard**
¾ **tsp. ground cinnamon**
¾ **tsp. ground cumin**

1. Preheat oven to 325°. Place the ham on a rack in a roasting pan. Using a sharp knife, score surface of ham with ½-in.-deep cuts in a diamond pattern. Bake, uncovered, 1½ hours.

2. Meanwhile, for glaze, in a small saucepan, mix brown sugar, honey, vinegar and ginger ale. Bring to a boil; cook until mixture is reduced by half, about 15 minutes. Stir in remaining ingredients. Reduce heat; simmer, uncovered, 5 minutes. Remove from heat. Reserve 1 cup mixture for sauce; keep warm.

3. Brush ham with some of the remaining glaze. Bake, uncovered, until a thermometer reads 140°, about 30 minutes, brushing twice with additional glaze. Serve with reserved sauce.

5 oz. cooked ham with 1 Tbsp. sauce: 270 cal., 6g fat (2g sat. fat), 100mg chol., 1234mg sod., 21g carb. (20g sugars, 0 fiber), 33g pro.

Baked Ham with Honey-Orange Glaze: Omit the glaze ingredients. Bake ham as directed. Meanwhile, combine ¼ cup packed brown sugar, ¼ cup orange juice, 2 Tbsp. honey, 1 Tbsp. stone-ground mustard, 2 tsp. dried basil, 1 tsp. orange zest and ⅛ tsp. ground cloves. Baste ham and proceed as recipe directs.

BEEF TACO LASAGNA

This crowd-friendly recipe makes two big 13x9 pans. Take both to the potluck...or keep one in the freezer to have an oven-ready dinner for your family another day.
—*Stacey Compton, Toledo, OH*

....

PREP: 30 min. • **BAKE:** 35 min. + standing • **MAKES:** 2 casseroles (8 servings each)

24 lasagna noodles
 2 lbs. lean ground beef (90% lean)
 2 envelopes taco seasoning
 4 large egg whites
 2 cartons (15 oz. each) ricotta cheese
 8 cups shredded cheddar cheese
 2 jars (24 oz. each) chunky salsa

1. Preheat oven to 350°. Cook noodles according to package directions. Meanwhile, in a large skillet, cook beef over medium heat until no longer pink; drain. Stir in taco seasoning. In a small bowl, combine egg whites and ricotta cheese. Drain noodles.

2. In each of two 13x9-in. baking dishes, layer 4 noodles, ⅔ cup ricotta mixture, half the beef mixture and 1⅓ cups cheddar cheese. Top each with 4 noodles, ⅔ cup ricotta mixture, 1⅓ cups salsa and 1⅓ cups cheese. For final layer, top each with 4 noodles, ⅔ cup ricotta mixture, 1⅓ cups salsa and 1⅓ cups cheese.

3. Bake, uncovered, 35-40 minutes or until heated through. Let stand for 10 minutes before cutting.

Freeze option: Cover and freeze unbaked lasagna. To use, partially thaw in refrigerator overnight. Remove from refrigerator 30 minutes before baking. Bake lasagna as directed, increasing the time as necessary to heat through and for a thermometer to read 165°.

1 piece: 545 cal., 26g fat (17g sat. fat), 109mg chol., 1198mg sod., 42g carb. (7g sugars, 1g fiber), 35g pro.

ITALIAN TURKEY SANDWICHES

My family loves the flavor of these shredded sandwiches from the slow cooker. They're perfect for a crowd, and any leftovers are just as good the next day.
—*Carol Riley, Ossian, IN*

PREP: 10 min. • **COOK:** 5 hours • **MAKES:** 12 sandwiches

1   bone-in turkey breast (6 lbs.), skin removed
1   medium onion, chopped
1   small green pepper, chopped
¼   cup chili sauce
3   Tbsp. white vinegar
2   Tbsp. dried oregano or Italian seasoning
4   tsp. beef bouillon granules
12 kaiser or hard rolls, split

1. Place turkey breast in a greased 5-qt. slow cooker. Add onion and green pepper.

2. Combine the chili sauce, vinegar, oregano and bouillon; pour over turkey and vegetables. Cover and cook on low for 5-6 hours or until turkey is tender.

3. Shred turkey with 2 forks and return to the slow cooker; heat through. Spoon ½ cup onto each roll.

Freeze option: Place the cooled meat and its juices in freezer containers. To use, partially thaw in the refrigerator overnight. Microwave, covered, on high in a microwave-safe dish until heated through, gently stirring and adding a little water if necessary.

1 sandwich: 374 cal., 4g fat (1g sat. fat), 118mg chol., 724mg sod., 34g carb. (3g sugars, 2g fiber), 49g pro. **Diabetic exchanges:** 6 lean meat, 2 starch.

GREEN CHILE CHICKEN CHILI

Jalapenos, green chiles and salsa verde guarantee spicy flavor in this chicken chili.
Tame the heat a bit by garnishing with a cool dollop of sour cream.
—*Fred Lockwood, Plano, TX*

PREP: 25 min. • **COOK:** 5 hours • **MAKES:** 10 servings (3½ qt.)

4 bone-in chicken breast halves (14 oz. each)

2 medium onions, chopped

2 medium green peppers, chopped

1 cup pickled jalapeno slices

1 can (4 oz.) chopped green chiles

2 jars (16 oz. each) salsa verde

2 cans (15½ oz. each) navy beans, rinsed and drained

1 cup sour cream

½ cup minced fresh cilantro

Optional toppings:
Shredded Colby-Monterey Jack cheese, sour cream and crushed tortilla chips

1. Place the chicken, onions, green peppers, jalapenos and chiles in a 5- or 6-qt. slow cooker. Pour salsa over top. Cover and cook on low 5-6 hours or until chicken is tender.

2. Remove chicken; cool slightly. Shred chicken with 2 forks, discarding skin and bones; return meat to slow cooker. Stir in the beans, sour cream and cilantro; heat through. Serve with toppings as desired.

Freeze option: Before adding sour cream, cilantro and toppings, cool chili. Freeze in freezer containers. To use, partially thaw in refrigerator overnight. Heat through in a saucepan, stirring occasionally and adding a little water if necessary. Stir in sour cream and cilantro. Serve with toppings as desired.

1⅓ cups: 320 cal., 7g fat (4g sat. fat), 79mg chol., 1187mg sod., 30g carb. (5g sugars, 7g fiber), 32g pro.

POTLUCK SPARERIBS

Love coming home from potlucks with an empty pan? Here's the recipe for you!
The tender, saucy ribs always disappear from a buffet table in minutes.

—*Sheri Kirkman, Lancaster, NY*

PREP: 10 min. • **BAKE:** 1¾ hours • **MAKES:** 12 servings

6 lbs. pork spareribs
1½ cups ketchup
¾ cup packed brown sugar
½ cup white vinegar
½ cup honey
⅓ cup soy sauce
1½ tsp. ground ginger
1 tsp. salt
¾ tsp. ground mustard
½ tsp. garlic powder
¼ tsp. pepper

1. Cut ribs into serving-sized pieces; place with the meaty side up on racks in 2 greased 13x9-in. baking pans. Cover tightly with foil. Bake at 350° for 1¼ hours or until meat is tender.

2. Remove racks; drain and return ribs to pans. Combine remaining ingredients; pour over ribs. Bake, uncovered, for 30-40 minutes or until the sauce coats ribs, basting occasionally. Ribs can also be grilled over medium-hot heat for the last 30-40 minutes instead of baking.

1 serving: 551 cal., 32g fat (12g sat. fat), 128mg chol., 1065mg sod., 34g carb. (28g sugars, 0 fiber), 32g pro.

TURKEY SLOPPY JOES FOR A CROWD

My mother's recipe box contained many hidden gems, including this one.
I like the meat mixture not only served on a bun, but also spooned over veggies.
—*Julie Clemes, Adrian, MI*

PREP: 25 min. • **COOK:** 40 min. • **MAKES:** 16 servings

3 lbs. lean ground turkey
3 medium green peppers, chopped
3 medium onions, finely chopped
2¼ cups ketchup
¾ cup water
3 Tbsp. white vinegar
3 Tbsp. spicy brown mustard
1 jalapeno pepper, seeded and chopped
½ tsp. pepper
16 whole wheat hamburger buns, split

1. In a Dutch oven coated with cooking spray, cook the turkey, green peppers and onions over medium heat until meat is no longer pink and vegetables are tender; drain.

2. Stir in the ketchup, water, vinegar, mustard, jalapeno and pepper. Bring to a boil. Reduce the heat; cover and simmer for 20-30 minutes, stirring occasionally. Serve on buns.

1 sandwich: 293 cal., 9g fat (2g sat. fat), 67mg chol., 751mg sod., 35g carb. (15g sugars, 4g fiber), 19g pro. **Diabetic exchanges:** 2 starch, 2 lean meat.

READER RAVE

"I've made these delicious sandwiches many times. If you're looking for an easy, last-minute recipe for a crowd, look no further. This is super simple and always a hit."
—SUMMY, TASTEOFHOME.COM

BAVARIAN POT ROAST

All my grandparents were German, so it's no wonder many of the recipes handed down to me are Bavarian. This traditional pot roast balances the tang of tomato and vinegar with cinnamon and ginger.
—*Susan Robertson, Hamilton, OH*

PREP: 15 min. • **COOK:** 2¾ hours • **MAKES:** 10 servings

1   boneless beef chuck pot roast (about 3 lbs.)
2   Tbsp. canola oil
1¼ cups water
¾   cup beer or beef broth
1   can (8 oz.) tomato sauce
½   cup chopped onion
2   Tbsp. sugar
1   Tbsp. vinegar
2   tsp. salt
1   tsp. ground cinnamon
1   bay leaf
½   tsp. pepper
½   tsp. ground ginger
    Optional: Cornstarch and water

1. In a Dutch oven, brown roast in hot oil. Combine water, beer, tomato sauce, onion, sugar, vinegar, salt, cinnamon, bay leaf, pepper and ginger. Pour over meat and bring to a boil. Reduce the heat; cover and simmer until meat is tender, 2½-3 hours.

2. Remove meat. Discard bay leaf. If desired, thicken juices with cornstarch and water.

Freeze option: Place sliced pot roast in freezer containers; top with cooking juices. Cool and freeze. To use, partially thaw in refrigerator overnight. Microwave, covered, on high in a microwave-safe dish until heated through, gently stirring and adding a little broth if necessary.

1 serving: 281 cal., 16g fat (5g sat. fat), 88mg chol., 633mg sod., 5g carb. (4g sugars, 0 fiber), 27g pro.

CHICKEN TATER BAKE

You'll please kids and adults alike with this irresistible comfort food.
It tastes like classic chicken potpie with a crispy Tater Tot crust. You can
even freeze the casseroles for up to three months.

—Fran Allen, St. Louis, MO

PREP: 20 min. • **BAKE:** 35 min. • **MAKES:** 2 casseroles (6 servings each)

2 cans (10¾ oz. each)
   condensed cream
   of chicken soup, undiluted
½ cup 2% milk
¼ cup butter, cubed
3 cups cubed cooked
   chicken
1 pkg. (16 oz.) frozen peas
   and carrots, thawed
1½ cups shredded cheddar
   cheese, divided
1 pkg. (32 oz.) frozen
   Tater Tots

1. In a large saucepan, combine soup, milk and butter. Cook and stir over medium heat until heated through. Remove from the heat; stir in chicken, peas and carrots, and 1 cup cheese.

2. Transfer to 2 greased 8-in. square baking dishes. Top with Tater Tots.

3. Bake at 400° until bubbling, 25-30 minutes. Sprinkle each casserole with ¼ cup cheese; bake until cheese is melted, about 5 minutes longer.

1 serving: 356 cal., 21g fat (9g sat. fat), 61mg chol., 844mg sod., 29g carb. (3g sugars, 4g fiber), 18g pro.

Beef Tater Bake: Do not make the chicken filling. Cook 2 pounds ground beef with 1 cup each chopped onion and celery; drain. Add 2 cans condensed cream of celery soup, 1 tsp. salt and ½ tsp. pepper. Place filling in baking dishes; proceed as directed.

POTLUCK TACO SALAD

I found this recipe in an old school cookbook, and I've taken it to many potlucks since then. The layers look so pretty in a glass bowl.
—*Sandy Fynaardt, New Sharon, IA*

TAKES: 25 min. • **MAKES:** 8 servings (1 cup dressing)

- 1 lb. ground beef
- 1 envelope taco seasoning, divided
- 1 medium head iceberg lettuce, torn
- 1 can (16 oz.) kidney beans, rinsed and drained
- 1 large red onion, chopped
- 4 medium tomatoes, seeded and finely chopped
- 2 cups shredded cheddar cheese
- 4 cups crushed tortilla chips (about 8 oz.)
- 1 bottle (8 oz.) Thousand Island salad dressing
- 2 Tbsp. taco sauce

1. In a large skillet, cook and crumble beef over medium heat until no longer pink, 6-8 minutes; drain. Stir in 3 Tbsp. taco seasoning.

2. In a large bowl, layer beef mixture, lettuce, beans, onion, tomatoes, cheese and crushed chips. In a small bowl, mix salad dressing, taco sauce and remaining taco seasoning; serve with salad.

1½ cups salad with 2 Tbsp. dressing: 574 cal., 34g fat (11g sat. fat), 66mg chol., 1109mg sod., 44g carb. (9g sugars, 5g fiber), 23g pro.

READER RAVE

"I've been making this salad for over 30 years—my family loves it! The only thing I changed was to use green goddess dressing instead of Thousand Island. But whatever kind you choose, the salad is delicious."

—TILLMANDEE, TASTEOFHOME.COM

ZIPPY CHICKEN ENCHILADAS

Leftover chicken will get an awesome makeover in this rich and creamy casserole. Loaded with flavor, it's a nice change of pace from enchiladas made with beef.
—Julie Moutray, Wichita, KS

PREP: 15 min. • **BAKE:** 35 min. • **MAKES:** 10 servings

1   can (16 oz.) refried beans
10 flour tortillas (8 in.), warmed
1   can (10¾ oz.) condensed cream of chicken soup, undiluted
1   cup sour cream
3   to 4 cups cubed cooked chicken
3   cups shredded cheddar cheese, divided
1   can (15 oz.) enchilada sauce
¼   cup sliced green onions
¼   cup sliced ripe olives
    Shredded lettuce, optional

1. Spread about 2 Tbsp. refried beans on each tortilla. Combine soup and sour cream; stir in chicken. Spoon ⅓-½ cup down center of each tortilla; top each with 1 Tbsp. cheese.

2. Roll up and place seam side down in a greased 13x9-in. baking dish. Pour enchilada sauce over top; sprinkle with the onions, olives and remaining cheese.

3. Bake, uncovered, at 350° for about 35 minutes or until heated through. Just before serving, sprinkle shredded lettuce around enchiladas if desired.

Freeze option: Cover and freeze unbaked casserole. To use, partially thaw in refrigerator overnight. Remove from refrigerator 30 minutes before baking. Preheat oven to 350°. Bake casserole as directed, increasing the time as necessary to heat through and for a thermometer inserted in center to read 165°.

1 serving: 487 cal., 23g fat (12g sat. fat), 95mg chol., 1001mg sod., 39g carb. (3g sugars, 4g fiber), 29g pro.

SLOW-COOKER KALUA PORK & CABBAGE

I think this tastes just like the kalua pork made in Hawaii that's slow-roasted all day in an underground oven. My simpler version requires only four ingredients and takes less than 10 minutes to prep.
—*Rholinelle DeTorres, San Jose, CA*

PREP: 10 min. • **COOK:** 9 hours • **MAKES:** 12 servings

7   bacon strips, divided
1   boneless pork shoulder butt roast (3 to 4 lbs.), well trimmed
1   Tbsp. coarse sea salt
1   medium head cabbage (about 2 lbs.), coarsely chopped

1. Line bottom of a 6-qt. slow cooker with four bacon strips. Sprinkle all sides of roast with salt; place in slow cooker. Arrange remaining bacon over top of roast.

2. Cook, covered, on low 8-10 hours or until the pork is tender. Add cabbage, spreading cabbage around roast. Cook, covered, 1-1¼ hours longer, until cabbage is tender.

3. Remove pork to a serving bowl; shred with 2 forks. Using a slotted spoon, add cabbage to pork and toss to combine. If desired, skim fat from some of the cooking juices; stir juices into pork mixture or serve on the side.

1 cup: 227 cal., 13g fat (5g sat. fat), 72mg chol., 622mg sod., 4g carb. (2g sugars, 2g fiber), 22g pro.

POTLUCK FRIED CHICKEN

This Sunday dinner staple is fried first, then baked to a crispy golden brown.
Seasoned with oregano and sage, it's sure to please at church potlucks and picnics.
—Donna Kuhaupt, Slinger, WI

PREP: 40 min. • **BAKE:** 25 min. • **MAKES:** 12 servings

1½ cups all-purpose flour
½ cup cornmeal
¼ cup cornstarch
3 tsp. salt
2 tsp. paprika
1 tsp. dried oregano
1 tsp. rubbed sage
1 tsp. pepper
2 large eggs
¼ cup water
2 broiler/fryer chickens (3 to 4 lbs. each), cut up
Oil for frying

1. In a large shallow dish, combine the flour, cornmeal, cornstarch, salt, paprika, oregano, sage and pepper. In a shallow bowl, beat eggs and water. Dip chicken in egg mixture; place in flour mixture, a few pieces at a time, and turn to coat.

2. In an electric skillet, heat 1 in. of oil to 375°. Fry the chicken, a few pieces at a time, until golden and crispy, 3-5 minutes on each side.

3. Place in 2 ungreased 15x10x1-in. baking pans. Bake, uncovered, at 350° until juices run clear, 25-30 minutes.

5 oz. cooked chicken: 497 cal., 29g fat (6g sat. fat), 135mg chol., 693mg sod., 20g carb. (0 sugars, 1g fiber), 36g pro.

TEST KITCHEN TIP

Cooking for children? This recipe can be used to make kid-friendly chicken strips and nuggets, too.

PUMPKIN
DOUGHNUT
DROPS, 222

CHAPTER 6

BIG BATCH DISHES

Feeding a huge crowd? It's as easy as can be when you rely on these large-yield appetizers, desserts and more!

CRANBERRY RUGELACH

These traditional Polish cookies keep well in an airtight container. Once I sent a batch to my sister, but the box got lost. She received it 12 days later—and said it was worth the wait!
—*Jean Doxon, Omaha, NE*

PREP: 25 min. + chilling • **BAKE:** 20 min./batch + cooling • **MAKES:** about 5 dozen

1 cup butter, softened
1 pkg. (8 oz.) cream cheese, softened
½ cup sugar
2¾ cups all-purpose flour
1 tsp. salt

FILLING

¾ cup sugar
⅔ cup dried cranberries, finely chopped
½ cup finely chopped walnuts, toasted
⅓ cup butter, melted
2 tsp. ground cinnamon
1 tsp. ground allspice
1 large egg, lightly beaten
Additional sugar

1. In a large bowl, cream softened butter, cream cheese and sugar until light and fluffy, 5-7 minutes. Combine flour and salt; gradually add to creamed mixture and mix well.

2. Turn onto a lightly floured surface; knead for 3 minutes or until smooth. Divide into 8 portions. Roll each portion into a ball; flatten into a 4-in. circle. Wrap and refrigerate at least 1 hour.

3. In a small bowl, combine sugar, cranberries, walnuts, melted butter, cinnamon and allspice. On a lightly floured surface, roll 1 portion of the dough into an 8-in. circle. Sprinkle with 3 Tbsp. of filling to within ½ in. of edges. Cut into 8 wedges.

4. Roll up wedges from the wide end and place point side down 2 in. apart on foil-lined baking sheets. Curve ends to form a crescent shape. Brush with egg; sprinkle with additional sugar.

5. Repeat with remaining dough and filling. Bake at 350° for 18-20 minutes or until golden brown. Remove to wire racks to cool.

1 cookie: 103 cal., 6g fat (3g sat. fat), 17mg chol., 80mg sod., 12g carb. (8g sugars, 0 fiber), 1g pro.

MUSHROOM & OLIVE BRUSCHETTA

I sampled these delicious appetizers at a party and knew I had to make them myself.
The original version used English muffins, but party rye or baguette slices work as well.
—*Lynne German, Buford, GA*

. . . .

PREP: 15 min. • **BAKE:** 10 min. • **MAKES:** 4 dozen

1½ **cups finely shredded cheddar cheese**

½ **cup canned mushroom stems and pieces, drained and chopped**

½ **cup chopped green onions**

½ **cup chopped pitted green olives**

½ **cup chopped ripe olives**

½ **cup mayonnaise**

¼ **tsp. curry powder**

2 **French bread baguettes (10½ oz. each), cut into ½-in. slices**

Julienned green onions, optional

1. Preheat oven to 400°. In a large bowl, combine the first 7 ingredients. Cut each baguette into 24 slices; place on ungreased baking sheets. Bake until lightly toasted, about 5 minutes.

2. Top with cheese mixture. Bake until cheese is melted, 4-5 minutes. If desired, top with julienned green onions.

Freeze option: Cover and freeze the unbaked topped baguette slices on a parchment-lined baking sheet until firm. Transfer to a freezer container; return to the freezer. To use, bake baguette slices on ungreased baking sheets in a preheated 400° oven until heated through, 8-10 minutes.

1 appetizer: 66 cal., 3g fat (1g sat. fat), 4mg chol., 161mg sod., 7g carb. (0 sugars, 0 fiber), 2g pro.

DIPPED CHERRY COOKIES

In our family, these festive little gems are a must for the holidays. We gave a batch to our mail carrier to thank her for trudging through the snow. She asked for the recipe!
—*Ruth Anne Dale, Titusville, PA*

PREP: 30 min. • **BAKE:** 10 min./batch + standing • **MAKES:** about 4 dozen

2½ cups all-purpose flour
¾ cup sugar, divided
1 cup cold butter, cubed
½ cup finely chopped maraschino cherries, patted dry
12 oz. white baking chocolate, finely chopped, divided
½ tsp. almond extract
2 tsp. shortening
Coarse sugar and red edible glitter

1. In a large bowl, combine flour and ½ cup sugar; cut in butter until crumbly. Knead in cherries, ⅔ cup white chocolate and extract until dough forms a ball.

2. Shape into ¾-in. balls. Place 2 in. apart on ungreased baking sheets. Flatten slightly with a glass dipped in the remaining sugar. Bake at 325° for 10-12 minutes or until the edges are lightly browned. Remove to wire racks to cool completely.

3. In a microwave, melt shortening and remaining white chocolate; stir until smooth.

4. Dip half of each cookie into chocolate; allow excess to drip off. Place on waxed paper; sprinkle with coarse sugar and edible glitter. Let stand until set. Store in an airtight container.

1 serving: 108 cal., 6g fat (4g sat. fat), 11mg chol., 34mg sod., 12g carb. (7g sugars, 0 fiber), 1g pro.

MINIATURE PEANUT BUTTER TREATS

I have three children and eight grandchildren. Every one of them loves these chocolate and peanut butter "thingies," as the grandkids like to call them!
—*Jodie McCoy, Tulsa, OK*

PREP: 20 min. + chilling • **BAKE:** 10 min./batch + cooling • **MAKES:** 3½ dozen

COOKIE

- ½ cup butter, softened
- ½ cup sugar
- ½ cup packed brown sugar
- 1 large egg, room temperature
- ½ cup creamy peanut butter
- ½ tsp. vanilla extract
- 1¼ cups all-purpose flour
- ¾ tsp. baking soda
- ½ tsp. salt

FILLING

- 42 miniature peanut butter-chocolate cups

1. In a bowl, combine the butter, sugars, egg, peanut butter and vanilla; beat until smooth. Combine the flour, baking soda and salt; gradually add to creamed mixture. Cover and chill for 1 hour or until easy to handle.

2. Roll into 42 walnut-sized balls; place in greased miniature muffin cups. Bake at 375° for 8-9 minutes.

3. Remove from oven; gently press 1 miniature peanut butter cup into each cookie, forming a depression. Cool for 10 minutes before removing to wire racks to cool completely.

1 piece: 108 cal., 6g fat (3g sat. fat), 11mg chol., 108mg sod., 12g carb. (9g sugars, 1g fiber), 2g pro.

READER RAVE

"You can never go wrong with peanut butter and chocolate. The hardest part of this recipe is unwrapping the peanut butter cups! So simple, so yummy."

—PAGERD, TASTEOFHOME.COM

MAKE-AHEAD SAUSAGE PINWHEELS

Meaty and cheesy, these simple roll-ups make a hearty snack. I like to assemble
the pinwheels well ahead of time and store them in the freezer.
On the day of the potluck, I just pop them in the oven.
—*Cindy Nerat, Menominee, MI*

. . . .

PREP: 30 min. + freezing • **BAKE:** 15 min. • **MAKES:** about 6½ dozen

1 lb. bulk regular or spicy pork sausage

½ cup diced sweet red pepper

1 green onion, chopped

1 pkg. (8 oz.) cream cheese, cubed

2 tubes (8 oz. each) refrigerated crescent rolls

1. Preheat oven to 350°. In a large skillet, cook and crumble sausage over medium-high heat until no longer pink, 5-7 minutes; drain. Add pepper and onion; cook and stir 2 minutes. Transfer to a bowl; cool 10 minutes. Stir in cream cheese until blended; cool completely.

2. Unroll 1 can of crescent dough and separate into 4 rectangles; pinch the perforations to seal. Press each rectangle to 6x4½ in.; spread each with ⅓ cup filling to within ¼ in. of edges. Roll up jelly-roll style, starting with a short side; pinch seam to seal. Roll gently to make logs smooth. Place on a waxed paper-lined baking sheet, seam side down. Repeat with remaining crescent dough. Freeze, covered, until firm, about 1 hour.

3. Cut each log into 10 slices. Bake on parchment-lined baking sheets until golden brown, 15-18 minutes. Serve while warm.

Freeze option: Freeze pinwheels in freezer containers, separating layers with waxed paper. To use, bake frozen pinwheels as directed, increasing time by 3-5 minutes.

1 appetizer: 46 cal., 3g fat (1g sat. fat), 6mg chol., 89mg sod., 2g carb. (1g sugars, 0 fiber), 1g pro.

CURRY-KISSED COCONUT FUDGE

Sugar and spice make everything nice—especially in this recipe! The creamy fudge is sprinkled with sweet curry powder for a delightfully different treat.
—*Sarah Meuser, New Milford, CT*

PREP: 25 min. + chilling • **MAKES:** about 4½ lbs.

- 2 tsp. plus ¼ cup butter, divided
- 4 pkg. (10 to 12 oz. each) white baking chips
- 2 cans (14 oz. each) sweetened condensed milk
- 1½ tsp. coconut extract
- ½ tsp. sea salt
- ¼ tsp. curry powder

1. Line a 13x9-in. pan with foil or parchment; grease foil with 2 tsp. butter.

2. In a large heavy saucepan, cook and stir baking chips, milk and remaining butter over low heat until smooth. Remove from heat; stir in extract and salt. Spread into prepared pan; sprinkle with curry powder. Refrigerate, covered, until firm, about 2 hours.

3. Using foil, lift fudge out of pan. Remove foil; cut fudge into 1-in. squares. Store in an airtight container in the refrigerator.

1 piece: 78 cal., 4g fat (3g sat. fat), 6mg chol., 29mg sod., 9g carb. (9g sugars, 0 fiber), 1g pro.

TEST KITCHEN TIP

Before the fudge sets up, sprinkle it with toasted coconut to add texture and even more coconut flavor.

CROWD-PLEASING PARTY MEATBALLS

We served these saucy baked meatballs at our wedding. They were such a hit, they've been in demand for other weddings and events ever since.

—Stefany Blevins, Portsmouth, OH

PREP: 30 min. • **BAKE:** 1 hour • **MAKES:** about 7 dozen

2 large eggs, lightly beaten
1 can (12 oz.) evaporated milk
2 cups quick-cooking oats
1 cup finely chopped onion
2 tsp. salt
2 tsp. chili powder
½ tsp. garlic powder
½ tsp. pepper
3 lbs. ground beef

SAUCE
2 cups ketchup
1½ cups packed brown sugar
½ cup chopped onion

1. In a large bowl, combine the first 8 ingredients. Crumble beef over mixture and mix well. Shape into 1-in. balls. Place in 3 greased 13x9-in. baking dishes.

2. Combine the sauce ingredients; pour over meatballs. Bake, uncovered, at 325° for 1 hour or until the meat is no longer pink.

1 meatball: 61 cal., 2g fat (1g sat. fat), 14mg chol., 148mg sod., 7g carb. (6g sugars, 0 fiber), 4g pro.

READER RAVE

"I've made these several times. The last time, I made more than 300 for my wedding. There wasn't a single meatball left! The only thing I've done differently is added a little barbecue sauce to the meat mixture. I froze the baked meatballs, and they traveled 400 miles in a cooler to go in a roaster with the barbecue sauce. Fantastic recipe!"

—TRACYV, TASTEOFHOME.COM

ROSEMARY SHORTBREAD COOKIES

With a hint of rosemary and classic buttery texture, these elegant cookies are melt-in-your-mouth scrumptious. The fact that they're easy to make can be your little secret!

—*Amavida Coffee, Rosemary Beach, FL*

PREP: 30 min. + chilling • **BAKE:** 15 min./batch • **MAKES:** 5½ dozen

1 cup butter, softened
½ cup confectioners' sugar
2 cups all-purpose flour
2 Tbsp. minced fresh rosemary
½ tsp. sea salt

1. In a large bowl, cream the butter and confectioners' sugar until light and fluffy. 5-7 minutes. Combine flour, rosemary and salt; gradually add to creamed mixture and mix well.

2. Shape the dough into two 8¼-in. rolls; wrap each in plastic. Refrigerate overnight. Cut into ¼-in. slices. Place 2 in. apart on ungreased baking sheets.

3. Bake at 350° for 11-13 minutes or until edges begin to brown. Cool for 1 minute before removing from pans to wire racks. Store in an airtight container.

1 serving: 42 cal., 3g fat (2g sat. fat), 7mg chol., 38mg sod., 4g carb. (1g sugars, 0 fiber), 0 pro.

TEST KITCHEN TIP

When slicing the roll of dough, rotate it a quarter-turn after each slice—this prevents the roll from flattening out into an oval as the dough warms and you apply pressure with each cut.

MINI GRILLED CHEESE

Looking for the perfect make-ahead snack? These little sandwiches are guaranteed to please. Keep some in the freezer for your family to enjoy with soup or salad.
—*Anita Curtis, Camarillo, CA*

TAKES: 30 min. • **MAKES:** 8 dozen

1 cup butter, softened
2 jars (5 oz. each) sharp American cheese spread, softened
1 large egg
1 can (4 oz.) chopped green chiles, drained
¼ cup salsa
2 cups shredded cheddar cheese
2 loaves (1½ lbs. each) thinly sliced sandwich bread, crusts removed

1. Preheat oven to 350°. Cream butter, cheese spread and egg until smooth. Stir in chiles, salsa and cheddar cheese. Spread about 1 Tbsp. cheese mixture on each slice of 1 loaf of bread.

2. Top with remaining bread; spread with more cheese mixture. Cut each sandwich into 4 squares or triangles; place on a baking sheet lined with parchment. Bake until cheese is melted, 10-15 minutes.

Freeze option: Place in a single layer on a baking sheet. Freeze 1 hour. Transfer to an airtight container and store in the freezer. Bake frozen appetizers as directed until bubbly and browned, about 15-20 minutes.

2 pieces: 102 cal., 7g fat (4g sat. fat), 22mg chol., 213mg sod., 8g carb. (1g sugars, 0 fiber), 3g pro.

POPPY SEED SQUARES

When I came across this unique recipe, I couldn't wait to try it. Now all my holiday menus include these savory bites. They're so tasty, they get snatched up in a flash.
—*Jo Baden, Independence, KS*

PREP: 35 min. • **BAKE:** 25 min. • **MAKES:** about 8 dozen

1 lb. ground beef
1½ cups finely chopped fresh mushrooms
1 medium onion, finely chopped
1 can (10¾ oz.) condensed cream of celery or mushroom soup, undiluted
1 Tbsp. prepared horseradish
1 tsp. salt
½ tsp. pepper

CRUST
3 cups all-purpose flour
2 Tbsp. poppy seeds
¾ tsp. baking powder
¾ tsp. salt
1 cup shortening
½ cup cold water

1. In a large skillet, cook the beef, mushrooms and onion over medium heat until meat is no longer pink, breaking into crumbles Add the soup, horseradish, salt and pepper. Remove from the heat; set aside.

2. In a large bowl, combine flour, poppy seeds, baking powder and salt. Cut in shortening until the mixture resembles coarse crumbs. Gradually add the cold water, tossing with a fork until a ball forms. Divide dough in half. Roll out 1 portion into a 15x10-in. rectangle; transfer to an ungreased 15x10x1-in. baking pan.

3. Spoon meat mixture over crust. Roll out the remaining dough into a 15x10-in. rectangle; place over filling. Bake at 425° until golden brown, about 25 minutes. Cut into small squares.

1 piece: 43 cal., 3g fat (1g sat. fat), 3mg chol., 50mg sod., 3g carb. (0 sugars, 0 fiber), 1g pro.

PORK & CHIVE POT STICKERS

Here's one of our favorite appetizers. My three kids love homemade pot stickers, which are more nutritious than many you find at restaurants.
—Marisa Raponi, Vaughan, ON

PREP: 1 hour • **COOK:** 5 min./batch • **MAKES:** 5 dozen

2 medium carrots, finely chopped
1 small onion, finely chopped
½ cup finely chopped water chestnuts
⅓ cup minced fresh chives
1 large egg white, lightly beaten
3 Tbsp. reduced-sodium soy sauce
½ tsp. pepper
1 lb. ground pork
60 pot sticker or gyoza wrappers
3 Tbsp. canola oil, divided
1 cup chicken broth, divided
Additional reduced-sodium soy sauce, optional

1. In a large bowl, combine the first 7 ingredients. Add pork; mix lightly but thoroughly. Place a scant 1 Tbsp. filling in center of each wrapper. (Cover the remaining wrappers with a damp paper towel until ready to use.)

2. Moisten wrapper edges with water. Fold wrapper over filling; seal edges, pleating the front side several times to form a pleated pouch. Stand pot stickers on a work surface to flatten bottoms; curve slightly to form crescent shapes, if desired.

3. In a large nonstick skillet, heat 1 Tbsp. canola oil over medium-high heat. Arrange a third of the pot stickers in concentric circles in the pan, flat side down; cook for 1-2 minutes or until bottoms are golden brown. Carefully add ⅓ cup chicken broth (broth may splatter); reduce heat to medium-low. Cook, covered, 2-3 minutes or until broth is almost absorbed and filling is cooked through.

4. Cook, uncovered, until bottoms are crisp and broth is completely evaporated, about 1 minute. Repeat with remaining oil, pot stickers and broth. If desired, serve with additional soy sauce.

1 pot sticker: 39 cal., 2g fat (0 sat. fat), 6mg chol., 66mg sod., 4g carb. (0 sugars, 0 fiber), 2g pro.

MINI PHYLLO TACOS

Tacos become one easy-to-eat bite when you load the seasoned beef and cheese into crispy phyllo cups. Hungry crowds can't resist!

—*Roseann Weston, Philipsburg, PA*

PREP: 30 min. • **BAKE:** 10 min. • **MAKES:** 2½ dozen

1 lb. lean ground beef (90% lean)
½ cup finely chopped onion
1 envelope taco seasoning
¾ cup water
1¼ cups shredded Mexican cheese blend, divided
2 pkg. (1.9 oz. each) frozen miniature phyllo tart shells

1. Preheat oven to 350°. In a small skillet, cook beef and onion over medium heat until meat is no longer pink, breaking into crumbles; drain. Stir in the taco seasoning and water. Bring to a boil. Reduce heat; simmer, uncovered, about 5 minutes. Remove from heat; stir in ½ cup cheese blend.

2. Place tart shells in an ungreased 15x10x1-in. baking pan. Fill with taco mixture.

3. Bake 6 minutes. Sprinkle with remaining cheese blend; bake until cheese is melted, 2-3 minutes longer.

Freeze option: Freeze cooled taco cups in a freezer container, separating layers with waxed paper. To use, reheat on a baking sheet in a preheated 350° oven until crisp and heated through.

1 appetizer: 63 cal., 3g fat (1g sat. fat), 11mg chol., 156mg sod., 4g carb. (0 sugars, 0 fiber), 4g pro.

CHOCOLATE HAZELNUT SHORTBREAD

We love hazelnut flavor and treats that aren't too sweet, so this shortbread is a winner in our family. For a sweeter version, turn the baked cutouts into sandwich cookies by spreading additional Nutella in between.
—*Karla Johnson, East Helena, MT*

PREP: 30 min. • **BAKE:** 10 min./batch + cooling • **MAKES:** about 7½ dozen

1 cup butter, softened
⅓ cup Nutella
1 cup confectioners' sugar
1 large egg, room temperature
3¾ cups all-purpose flour
1 tsp. ground cinnamon
Dash salt
½ cup finely chopped hazelnuts
Additional confectioners' sugar, optional

1. Preheat oven to 350°. Cream butter, Nutella and confectioners' sugar until light and fluffy, 5-7 minutes. Beat in egg. In another bowl, whisk flour, cinnamon and salt; gradually beat into creamed mixture. Add hazelnuts; mix well.

2. Divide dough in half; shape each into a disk. On a lightly floured surface, roll each portion to ⅛-in. thickness. Cut with a floured 2¼-in. scalloped round cookie cutter. Place 1 in. apart on ungreased baking sheets. Bake until the bottoms are light brown, 8-10 minutes. Remove from the pans to wire racks to cool. If desired, dust with confectioners' sugar.

1 cookie: 51 cal., 3g fat (1g sat. fat), 7mg chol., 33mg sod., 6g carb. (2g sugars, 0 fiber), 1g pro.

CHICKEN BACON TRIANGLES

I whip up a new menu item every year for our Christmas party. These were a hit!
—Annette Fecht, Surrento, BC

PREP: 60 min. + chilling • **BAKE:** 15 min. • **MAKES:** 4 dozen

½ lb. bacon strips, chopped

¾ lb. boneless skinless chicken breasts, cubed

½ cup condensed cream of mushroom soup, undiluted

4 oz. cream cheese, cubed

2 garlic cloves, minced

1½ tsp. dried minced onion

⅛ tsp. pepper

1 cup shredded part-skim mozzarella cheese

½ cup shredded Parmesan cheese

24 sheets phyllo dough, 14x9 in.

¼ cup butter, melted
Ranch dip, optional

1. In a large skillet, cook the bacon over medium heat until crisp. Remove to paper towels with a slotted spoon; drain, reserving drippings. Saute chicken in drippings until no longer pink; drain.

2. Add the soup, cream cheese, garlic, onion, pepper and bacon to skillet; cook and stir until blended. Remove from the heat. Stir in mozzarella and Parmesan cheeses; cool slightly. Cover and refrigerate for at least 2 hours.

3. Lightly brush 1 sheet of phyllo dough with butter; place another sheet on top and brush with butter. (Keep the remaining phyllo covered with a damp towel to prevent it from drying out.) Cut into four 14x2¼-in. strips.

4. Place a scant 1 Tbsp. filling on the lower corner of each strip. Fold dough over filling, forming a triangle. Fold triangle up, then fold triangle over, forming another triangle. Continue folding, like a flag, until you come to the end of the strip. Brush the end of dough with butter and press onto triangle to seal. Repeat with remaining strips of dough and with remaining sheets of phyllo.

5. Place triangles on a greased baking sheet. Bake at 375° until golden brown, 15-17 minutes. If desired, serve with ranch dip.

1 appetizer: 70 cal., 5g fat (2g sat. fat), 13mg chol., 121mg sod., 4g carb. (0 sugars, 0 fiber), 3g pro.

CARDAMOM BRAID BREAD

I found this recipe more than 35 years ago and have been making it for special occasions ever since. The glossy, golden brown braid is almost too pretty to eat.
—Rita Bergman, Olympia, WA

PREP: 30 min. + rising • **BAKE:** 20 min. • **MAKES:** 2 loaves (20 slices each)

6   cups all-purpose flour
2   pkg. (¼ oz. each) active dry yeast
1½   tsp. ground cardamom
1   tsp. salt
1½   cups plus 2 Tbsp. 2% milk, divided
½   cup butter, cubed
½   cup honey
2   large eggs, room temperature
2   Tbsp. sugar

1. In a large bowl, combine 2 cups flour, yeast, cardamom and salt. In a small saucepan, heat 1½ cups milk, butter and honey to 120°-130°. Add to the dry ingredients; beat just until moistened. Add eggs; beat until smooth. Stir in enough remaining flour to form a firm dough (dough will be sticky).

2. Turn onto a floured surface; knead until smooth and elastic, 6-8 minutes. Place in a greased bowl, turning once to grease top. Cover and let rise in a warm place until doubled, about 45 minutes.

3. Punch dough down. Turn onto a lightly floured surface; divide in half. Divide each portion into thirds. Shape each into a 14-in. rope. Place 3 ropes on a greased baking sheet and braid; pinch the ends to seal and tuck under. Repeat with remaining dough. Cover and let rise until doubled, about 30 minutes.

4. Brush with remaining milk and sprinkle with sugar. Bake at 375° until golden brown, 20-25 minutes. Remove from pans to wire racks to cool.

1 slice: 114 cal., 3g fat (2g sat. fat), 18mg chol., 91mg sod., 19g carb. (5g sugars, 1g fiber), 3g pro.

ANTIPASTO SALAD

I toss traditional antipasto ingredients with spiral pasta for a tasty crowd-pleaser. Guests rave about the homemade dressing, which is a nice alternative to bottled Italian.
—*Linda Harrington, Windham, NH*

PREP: 50 minutes + chilling • **COOK:** 10 min. • **MAKES:** 50 servings

- 2 pkg. (1 lb. each) spiral pasta
- 4 to 5 large tomatoes, chopped
- 3 large onions, chopped
- 2 large green peppers, chopped
- 2 cans (15 to 16 oz. each) garbanzo beans or chickpeas, rinsed and drained
- 1 lb. thinly sliced Genoa salami, julienned
- 1 lb. sliced pepperoni, julienned
- ½ lb. provolone cheese, cubed
- 1 cup pitted ripe olives, halved

DRESSING
- 1 cup red wine vinegar
- ½ cup sugar
- 2 Tbsp. dried oregano
- 2 tsp. salt
- 1 tsp. pepper
- 1½ cups olive oil

1. Cook pasta according to package directions. Drain; rinse with cold water. In several large bowls, combine pasta with next 8 ingredients.

2. For dressing, pulse vinegar, sugar, oregano, salt and pepper in a blender. While processing, gradually add the olive oil in a steady stream. Pour over salad; toss to coat. Refrigerate, covered, 4 hours or overnight.

¾ cup: 214 cal., 15g fat (4g sat. fat), 19mg chol., 514mg sod., 13g carb. (4g sugars, 1g fiber), 7g pro.

READER RAVE

"Wow, was this good! When I used mozzarella instead of provolone, the salad still turned out great. The recipe is easy to cut in half, too."

—KARINW64, TASTEOFHOME.COM

PUMPKIN DOUGHNUT DROPS

When my grandchildren visit, I make sure to have special treats on hand.
I see lots of smiles when I bring out a platter of these yummy cake doughnuts.
—*Beva Staum, Muscoda, WI*

PREP: 10 min. • **COOK:** 5 min./batch • **MAKES:** about 7 dozen

2 large eggs
1¼ cups sugar
2 Tbsp. shortening
1 cup canned pumpkin
2 tsp. white vinegar
1 tsp. vanilla extract
3 cups all-purpose flour
½ cup nonfat dry milk powder
3 tsp. baking powder
½ tsp. salt
½ tsp. ground cinnamon
½ tsp. ground nutmeg
½ cup lemon-lime soda
Oil for deep-fat frying
Additional sugar

1. In a large bowl, beat eggs, sugar and shortening until blended. Beat in pumpkin, vinegar and vanilla. In another bowl, whisk together flour, milk powder, baking powder, salt and spices. Add to egg mixture alternately with soda, beating after each addition.

2. In a deep cast-iron skillet or deep-fat fryer, heat oil to 375°. Drop teaspoonfuls of batter, a few at a time, into hot oil. Fry until golden brown, about 1 minute per side. Drain on paper towels. Roll in additional sugar while warm.

1 doughnut: 48 cal., 2g fat (0 sat. fat), 5mg chol., 36mg sod., 7g carb. (3g sugars, 0 fiber), 1g pro.

TEST KITCHEN TIP

If you like, roll the fried doughnuts in a cinnamon-sugar mixture or sifted confectioners' sugar instead of plain granulated sugar.

ZUCCHINI APPLE BREAD

Early autumn means zucchini is taking off in the garden and fresh apples are plentiful. I put both to great use in a tender, nutty quick bread.
—*Kathy Strawser, Dunkirk, NY*

. . . .

PREP: 30 min. • **BAKE:** 55 min. + cooling • **MAKES:** 3 loaves (12 slices each)

4 cups all-purpose flour
3 tsp. baking soda
1½ tsp. ground cinnamon
½ tsp. ground nutmeg
¼ tsp. salt
5 large eggs, room temperature
1½ cups vegetable oil
2 cups sugar
1 cup packed brown sugar
1 tsp. vanilla extract
2 cups shredded zucchini
1½ cups chopped pecans
1 cup grated peeled apples

1. In a large bowl, combine flour, baking soda, cinnamon, nutmeg and salt. In a large bowl, beat eggs until frothy. Add oil, sugars and vanilla; beat until blended. Stir into dry ingredients just until moistened. Fold in zucchini, pecans and apples.

2. Transfer to 3 greased 8x4-in. loaf pans. Bake at 350° until a toothpick inserted in the center comes out clean, 55-60 minutes. Cool for 10 minutes before removing from pans to wire racks.

1 slice: 246 cal., 14g fat (2g sat. fat), 30mg chol., 133mg sod., 29g carb. (18g sugars, 1g fiber), 3g pro.

READER RAVE

"I've been making this for years. My whole family loves it! The bread turns out flavorful and moist. It also freezes well and tastes just as good from the freezer as it does freshly baked. I add walnuts because my husband likes them."
—MANDY257, TASTEOFHOME.COM

CHOCOLATE CARAMEL
KISS COOKIES, 248

CHAPTER 7

SWEET TREATS

Everyone saves room for dessert when these special sweets are on the buffet table. Go ahead—indulge!

PECAN PIE COBBLER

When I couldn't find just the right dessert recipe, I came up with my own
that combines the ease of a cobbler with the richness of pecan pie.
Add a scoop of ice cream or a dollop of whipped cream on top.
—*Willa Kelley, Edmond, OK*

PREP: 20 min. • **BAKE:** 30 min. + cooling • **MAKES:** 12 servings

½ cup butter, cubed
1 cup plus 2 Tbsp.
   all-purpose flour
¾ cup sugar
3 tsp. baking powder
¼ tsp. salt
⅔ cup 2% milk
1 tsp. vanilla extract
1½ cups coarsely chopped
   pecans
1 cup packed brown sugar
¾ cup brickle toffee bits
1½ cups boiling water
   Vanilla ice cream, optional

1. Preheat oven to 350°. Place butter in a 13x9-in. baking pan; heat pan in oven 3-5 minutes or until the butter is melted. Meanwhile, combine the flour, sugar, baking powder and salt. Stir in milk and vanilla until combined.

2. Remove baking pan from oven; add batter. Sprinkle with pecans, brown sugar and toffee bits. Slowly pour boiling water over the top (do not stir). Bake, uncovered, until golden brown, 30-35 minutes. Cool on wire rack for 30 minutes (cobbler will thicken upon cooling). Serve warm, with ice cream if desired.

1 serving: 411 cal., 23g fat (8g sat. fat), 26mg chol., 327mg sod., 51g carb. (41g sugars, 2g fiber), 3g pro.

READER RAVE

"This was the featured dessert at a farm-to-table dinner I helped organize. We served the cobbler to showcase local pecans—what a wonderful way to do it! I didn't change the recipe at all and definitely recommend ice cream on top."

—MELISSA, TASTEOFHOME.COM

JELLY DOUGHNUTS

Why run to the bakery when you crave jelly doughnuts? These goodies are lighter than air and easier to make than you might think. I've been serving them for many years, and they disappear almost as quickly as I set them out.

—*Kathy Westendorf, Westgate, IA*

PREP: 30 min. • **COOK:** 10 min. • **MAKES:** 16 doughnuts

2 pkg. (¼ oz. each) active dry yeast
½ cup warm water (110° to 115°)
½ cup warm 2% milk (110° to 115°)
⅓ cup butter, softened
1⅓ cups sugar, divided
3 large egg yolks, room temperature
1 tsp. salt
3 to 3¾ cups all-purpose flour
3 Tbsp. jelly or jam
1 large egg white, lightly beaten
Oil for deep-fat frying

1. In a small bowl, dissolve yeast in warm water. In a large bowl, combine milk, butter, ⅓ cup sugar, egg yolks, salt, yeast mixture and 3 cups flour; beat until smooth. Stir in enough remaining flour to form a soft dough (do not knead).

2. Place in a greased bowl, turning once to grease top. Cover and let rise in a warm place until doubled, about 45 minutes.

3. Punch dough down. Turn onto a lightly floured surface; knead about 10 times. Divide dough in half.

4. Roll each portion to ¼-in. thickness; cut with a floured 2½-in. round cutter. Place about ½ tsp. jelly in the center of half of the circles; brush edges with egg white. Top with remaining circles; press edges to seal tightly. Place on greased baking sheet. Cover and let rise until doubled, about 45 minutes.

5. In an electric skillet or deep-fat fryer, heat oil to 375°. Fry doughnuts, a few at a time, 1-2 minutes on each side or until golden brown. Drain on paper towels. Roll warm doughnuts in remaining sugar.

1 doughnut: 270 cal., 12g fat (3g sat. fat), 45mg chol., 188mg sod., 38g carb. (19g sugars, 1g fiber), 4g pro.

CANDY BAR BROWNIES

Chocolate lovers, rejoice! Two kinds of candy bars go into these chunky homemade brownies, making them especially rich and decadent.
—*Sharon Evans, Clear Lake, IA*

PREP: 15 min. • **BAKE:** 30 min. + cooling • **MAKES:** 3 dozen

- ¾ cup butter, melted
- 2 cups sugar
- 4 large eggs, room temperature
- 2 tsp. vanilla extract
- 1½ cups all-purpose flour
- ⅓ cup baking cocoa
- ½ tsp. baking powder
- ¼ tsp. salt
- 4 Snickers bars (2.07 oz. each), cut into ¼-in. pieces
- 3 plain milk chocolate candy bars (1.55 oz. each), coarsely chopped

1. In a large bowl, combine butter, sugar, eggs and vanilla. In a small bowl, combine flour, cocoa, baking powder and salt; set aside ¼ cup. Stir remaining dry ingredients into the egg mixture until well combined. Toss Snickers pieces with reserved flour mixture; stir into batter.

2. Transfer to a greased 13x9-in. baking pan. Sprinkle with milk chocolate candy bar pieces. Bake at 350° for 30-35 minutes or until a toothpick inserted in the center comes out clean (do not overbake). Cool on a wire rack. Chill before cutting.

1 brownie: 121 cal., 5g fat (3g sat. fat), 34mg chol., 73mg sod., 17g carb. (12g sugars, 0 fiber), 2g pro.

READER RAVE

"I made these for my dad's Father's Day picnic. They were super easy and everyone loved them. The batter divides nicely into two 9-inch baking pans as well."

—DANIELLEYLEE, TASTEOFHOME.COM

MINI SWEET POTATO PIES

I'll always remember the day my 2-year-old son helped me create these yummy little treats. It was the first time he told me, "I love you!"
—*Emily Butler, South Williamsport, PA*

PREP: 45 minutes • **BAKE:** 25 min. + cooling • **MAKES:** 2 dozen

2 large sweet potatoes, peeled and cut into ¾-in. cubes
2 sheets refrigerated pie crust
¼ cup all-purpose flour
3 Tbsp. cold unsalted butter, cubed
1 cup packed brown sugar, divided

1. Preheat oven to 400°. Place the sweet potatoes in a greased 15x10x1-in. baking pan; bake until tender, 35-40 minutes.

2. Meanwhile, on a work surface, unroll 1 crust. Using a 2½-in. round cutter, cut out 12 circles. Press circles onto bottoms and up sides of 12 nonstick mini muffin cups. Repeat with second crust. Chill until filling is ready.

3. In a food processor, pulse flour, butter and ¼ cup brown sugar until crumbly; set aside for the topping. Add baked sweet potatoes and remaining brown sugar to food processor; pulse until almost smooth. Fill the crust-lined cups three-fourths full. Sprinkle with topping.

4. Decrease oven setting to 325°. Bake until the crust is golden brown, 20-24 minutes. Cool 5-10 minutes before removing from pan to a wire rack.

1 mini pie: 156 cal., 6g fat (3g sat. fat), 7mg chol., 67mg sod., 25g carb. (12g sugars, 1g fiber), 1g pro.

SALTED CASHEW & CARAMEL CHEWS

These chocolate-drizzled cookies made with caramel ice cream topping and sprinkled with nuts are impossible to resist. Just add a cold glass of milk—*mmm*, heaven.
—*Paula Marchesi, Lenhartsville, PA*

PREP: 25 min. • **BAKE:** 10 min./batch + cooling • **MAKES:** about 3 dozen

¾ cup unsalted butter, softened
1½ cups packed brown sugar
2 large eggs, room temperature
¼ cup hot caramel ice cream topping
1 tsp. vanilla extract
2½ cups all-purpose flour
¾ tsp. baking soda
¼ tsp. salt
2 cups semisweet chocolate chips, divided
1¼ cups lightly salted cashews, divided

1. Preheat oven to 350°. In a large bowl, cream butter and brown sugar until light and fluffy, 5-7 minutes. Gradually beat in eggs, caramel ice cream topping and vanilla. In another bowl, whisk flour, baking soda and salt; gradually beat into the creamed mixture. Stir in 1⅓ cups chocolate chips and ¾ cup cashews.

2. Drop cookie dough by rounded tablespoonfuls 2 in. apart onto parchment-lined baking sheets. Bake until edges are firm, 10-12 minutes. Cool on pans 5 minutes. Remove to wire racks to cool completely.

3. In a microwave, melt the remaining chocolate chips; stir until smooth. Drizzle over cookies; sprinkle with remaining cashews. Let stand until set.

1 cookie: 184 cal., 9g fat (5g sat. fat), 21mg chol., 68mg sod., 24g carb. (14g sugars, 1g fiber), 3g pro.

CLASSIC CHOCOLATE CAKE

This time-tested recipe appeared on a can of Hershey's cocoa in 1943. When I tried the cake, my boys devoured every bite, and I've been making it ever since. It's still one of the best.
—*Betty Follas, Morgan Hill, CA*

PREP: 15 min. • **BAKE:** 35 min. • **MAKES:** 15 servings

⅔ cup butter, softened
1⅔ cups sugar
3 large eggs, room temperature
2 cups all-purpose flour
⅔ cup baking cocoa
1¼ tsp. baking soda
1 tsp. salt
1⅓ cups whole milk
Confectioners' sugar or favorite frosting

1. In a bowl, cream butter and sugar until light and fluffy, 5-7 minutes. Add eggs, 1 at a time, beating well after each addition. Combine flour, cocoa, baking soda and salt; add to creamed mixture alternately with milk, beating until smooth after each addition. Pour batter into a greased and floured 13x9-in. baking pan.

2. Bake at 350° until a toothpick inserted in the center comes out clean, 35-40 minutes. Cool on a wire rack. When cake is cool, dust with confectioners' sugar or top with your favorite frosting.

1 piece: 257 cal., 10g fat (6g sat. fat), 67mg chol., 368mg sod., 38g carb. (23g sugars, 1g fiber), 4g pro.

NO-BAKE CEREAL COOKIE BARS

I pack these treats full of goodies, including raisins, oats and coconut. For extra color, sprinkle the M&M's onto the cereal mixture after it's in the pan, then press them in.
—Connie Craig, Lakewood, WA

....

PREP: 10 min. • **COOK:** 15 min. + cooling • **MAKES:** 3 dozen

4½ cups Rice Krispies
3¼ cups quick-cooking oats
½ cup cornflakes
½ cup sweetened shredded coconut
½ cup butter, cubed
1 pkg. (16 oz.) miniature marshmallows
¼ cup honey
½ cup M&M's minis
¼ cup raisins

1. Grease a 15x10x1-in. pan. In a large bowl, combine first 4 ingredients.

2. In a large saucepan, melt the butter over low heat. Add marshmallows; stir until completely melted. Stir in honey until blended. Pour over cereal mixture; stir until evenly coated. Cool 5 minutes.

3. Stir in M&M's and raisins; press into prepared pan using a greased spatula. Let stand 30 minutes before cutting. Store between layers of waxed paper in an airtight container.

1 bar: 137 cal., 4g fat (3g sat. fat), 8mg chol., 58mg sod., 24g carb. (13g sugars, 1g fiber), 2g pro. **Diabetic exchanges:** 1½ starch, ½ fat.

Health Tip: The M&M's minis add only 15 calories per serving. Go ahead and include those colorful candies to make your bars a little more eye-catching and fun.

CHOCOLATE PEAR HAZELNUT TART

As a newly arrived foreign exchange student in France, I was really homesick.
Then my host family's grandmother asked me to help her make this exquisite tart.
When I did, we formed a bond that needed no words. The art of baking transcends language!
—Lexi McKeown, Los Angeles, CA

PREP: 45 min. + chilling • **BAKE:** 30 min. + cooling • **MAKES:** 12 servings

1¼ cups all-purpose flour
⅓ cup ground hazelnuts
¼ cup packed brown sugar
Dash salt
½ cup cold butter, cubed
3 to 5 Tbsp. ice water

FILLING

3 large eggs, separated
⅓ cup butter, softened
⅓ cup packed brown sugar
2 Tbsp. amaretto or ½ tsp. almond extract
1 cup ground hazelnuts
2 Tbsp. baking cocoa
6 canned pear halves, drained, sliced and patted dry
2 Tbsp. honey, warmed
Confectioners' sugar, optional

1. Mix flour, hazelnuts, brown sugar and salt; cut in butter until crumbly. Gradually add ice water, tossing with a fork until the dough holds together when pressed. Shape into a disk. Wrap and refrigerate 30 minutes or overnight.

2. Place egg whites in a large bowl; let stand at room temperature 30 minutes. Preheat oven to 400°. On a lightly floured surface, roll dough to a ⅛-in.-thick circle; transfer to a 9-in. fluted tart pan with removable bottom. Trim crust even with edge. Prick bottom of crust with a fork. Refrigerate while preparing filling.

3. In a large bowl, cream butter and brown sugar until blended. Beat in egg yolks and amaretto. Beat in ground hazelnuts and cocoa.

4. With clean beaters, beat egg whites on medium speed until stiff peaks form. Fold a third of the egg whites into hazelnut mixture, then fold in remaining whites. Spread onto bottom of crust. Arrange pears over top.

5. Bake on a lower oven rack 30-35 minutes or until crust is golden brown. Brush pears with honey. Cool on a wire rack. If desired, dust with confectioners' sugar.

1 slice: 302 cal., 19g fat (9g sat. fat), 86mg chol., 125mg sod., 29g carb. (15g sugars, 2g fiber), 5g pro.

MALTED MILK CAKE

With crushed malted milk balls on top, this from-scratch cake always goes quickly.
I love the combination of sweet and salty, so sometimes I replace the candy with popcorn.
—*Susan Scarborough, Fernandina Beach, FL*

. . . .

PREP: 30 min. • **BAKE:** 20 min. + cooling • **MAKES:** 15 servings

1 cup butter, softened
1 cup sugar
4 large eggs, room temperature
½ tsp. butter flavoring, optional
2⅓ cups all-purpose flour
1 cup malted milk powder
2 tsp. baking powder
½ tsp. salt
⅔ cup whole milk

FROSTING

⅓ cup butter, softened
2¾ cups confectioners' sugar
⅓ cup baking cocoa
⅓ cup whole milk
1½ cups coarsely crushed malted milk balls

1. Preheat oven to 350°. Grease a 13x9-in. baking pan. In a large bowl, cream butter and sugar until light and fluffy, 5-7 minutes. Add eggs, 1 at a time, beating well after each addition. Batter may appear curdled. If desired, beat in butter flavoring. In another bowl, whisk flour, milk powder, baking powder and salt; add to creamed mixture alternately with milk, beating well after each addition.

2. Transfer batter to prepared pan. Bake 18-22 minutes or until a toothpick inserted in center comes out clean. Cool completely in pan on a wire rack.

3. In a large bowl, beat the butter until creamy. Beat in confectioners' sugar and cocoa alternately with milk until smooth. Spread frosting over cake; sprinkle with crushed malted milk balls.

1 piece: 455 cal., 20g fat (13g sat. fat), 95mg chol., 352mg sod., 65g carb. (46g sugars, 1g fiber), 5g pro.

SWEET POTATO CREAM CHEESE BARS

Need a dessert for an autumn potluck? These sweet potato bars are a yummy alternative to pumpkin. Feel free to make them ahead—they're even better refrigerated overnight.
—*Debbie Glasscock, Conway, AR*

PREP: 20 min. • **BAKE:** 45 min. + chilling • **MAKES:** 2 dozen

1 pkg. white cake mix (regular size)
1 cup chopped pecans, toasted
½ cup cold butter, cubed
1 pkg. (8 oz.) cream cheese, softened
½ cup sugar
3 large eggs, room temperature
1 can (14 oz.) sweetened condensed milk, divided
3 cups cooked and mashed sweet potatoes (about 3 medium)
2 tsp. pumpkin pie spice

1. Preheat oven to 350°. Combine cake mix and pecans; cut in butter until crumbly. Press mixture onto bottom of a greased 13x9-in. baking dish.

2. Beat the cream cheese, sugar, 1 egg and 2 Tbsp. milk until smooth; set aside. Stir together sweet potatoes, remaining eggs, remaining milk and pie spice; pour over pecan mixture. Dollop cream cheese mixture over sweet potato mixture. Cut through cream cheese mixture with a knife to swirl into sweet potato mixture.

3. Bake until set and slightly golden on top, about 45 minutes. Allow to cool completely; chill before cutting into bars.

1 bar: 304 cal., 15g fat (7g sat. fat), 51mg chol., 240mg sod., 40g carb. (27g sugars, 1g fiber), 5g pro.

TEST KITCHEN TIP

To cook your sweet potatoes, try using an electric pressure cooker—it takes just 10 minutes at high pressure. Or microwave the sweet potatoes, covered, for 8-10 minutes. For either method, be sure to pierce potatoes with a fork 4-5 times before cooking.

CHOCOLATE CARAMEL KISS COOKIES

Here's a fun twist on the classic peanut butter blossom. Cinnamon spices up the batter, and a caramel kiss goes on top. I make these with my family every Christmas.
—*Kristen Heigl, Staten Island, NY*

PREP: 15 min. • **BAKE:** 10 min./batch + cooling • **MAKES:** about 2 dozen

½ cup butter, softened
½ cup packed brown sugar
1 cup sugar, divided
1 large egg plus 1 large egg yolk, room temperature
1½ tsp. vanilla extract
1¼ cups all-purpose flour
¾ cup baking cocoa
1 tsp. baking soda
1 tsp. ground cinnamon
¾ tsp. salt
24 caramel-filled milk chocolate kisses

1. Preheat oven to 350°. Cream butter, brown sugar and ½ cup sugar until light and fluffy. Beat in the egg, egg yolk and vanilla. In another bowl, whisk the next 5 ingredients; gradually beat into creamed mixture.

2. Shape rounded tablespoons of dough into balls. Roll in the remaining sugar. Place 2 in. apart on ungreased baking sheets. Bake until the edges begin to brown, 8-10 minutes. Immediately press a chocolate kiss into center of each cookie (cookie will crack around edges). Cool on pans 2 minutes. Remove to wire racks to cool.

1 cookie: 143 cal., 6g fat (3g sat. fat), 27mg chol., 170mg sod., 23g carb. (15g sugars, 1g fiber), 2g pro.

SOUR CREAM POUND CAKE

This rich pound cake is beautiful dusted with sugar and filled with fruit in the center.
Or top individual slices with ice cream and chocolate syrup for a "sundae!"
—*Karen Conrad, East Troy, WI*

PREP: 15 min. • **BAKE:** 1¼ hours + cooling • **MAKES:** 20 servings

1   **cup butter, softened**
3   **cups sugar**
6   **large eggs, room temperature**
3   **cups all-purpose flour**
¼   **tsp. baking soda**
¼   **tsp. salt**
1   **cup sour cream**
2   **tsp. vanilla extract**
    Confectioners' sugar, optional

1. In a bowl, cream the butter and sugar until light and fluffy, 5-7 minutes. Add eggs, 1 at a time, beating well after each addition. Combine flour, baking soda and salt; add to creamed mixture alternately with sour cream and vanilla. Beat on low just until blended. Pour into a greased and floured 10-in. fluted tube pan.

2. Bake at 325° for 1¼-1½ hours or until a toothpick comes out clean. Cool in pan for 15 minutes before removing to a wire rack to cool completely. Sprinkle with confectioners' sugar if desired.

1 piece: 311 cal., 13g fat (7g sat. fat), 96mg chol., 163mg sod., 45g carb. (30g sugars, 1g fiber), 4g pro.

TEST KITCHEN TIP

Experiment with different fruit and nut combinations to decorate this pound cake. For exampe, try peaches and pecans; apples and walnuts; pineapple and macadamia nuts; or cherries and almonds.

KEY LIME CREAM PIE

This luscious no-bake dessert is cool and refreshing—perfect for summer potlucks. I always go home with an empty pie plate and lots of recipe requests.
—*Shirley Rickis, The Villages, FL*

PREP: 40 min. + chilling • **MAKES:** 12 servings

1 pkg. (11.3 oz.) pecan shortbread cookies, crushed (about 2 cups)
⅓ cup butter, melted
4 cups heavy whipping cream
¼ cup confectioners' sugar
1 tsp. coconut extract
1 pkg. (8 oz.) cream cheese, softened
1 can (14 oz.) sweetened condensed milk
½ cup Key lime juice
¼ cup sweetened shredded coconut, toasted
Optional: Maraschino cherries with stems and sliced Key limes

1. In a small bowl, mix the crushed shortbread cookies and butter. Press onto bottom and up sides of a greased 9-in. deep-dish pie plate. In a large bowl, beat cream until it begins to thicken. Add confectioners' sugar and coconut extract; beat until stiff peaks form. In another large bowl, beat cream cheese, condensed milk and lime juice until blended. Fold in 2 cups whipped cream. Spoon into the prepared crust.

2. Top with remaining whipped cream; sprinkle with toasted coconut. Refrigerate until serving, at least 4 hours. If desired, garnish with cherries and limes.

1 piece: 646 cal., 52g fat (30g sat. fat), 143mg chol., 252mg sod., 41g carb. (29g sugars, 0 fiber), 8g pro.

RECIPE INDEX